PowerXL Grill Air Fryer Combo Cookbook

1000 Days of Easy, Healthy PowerXL Grill Air Fryer Combo Recipes for Beginners and Advanced Users | Fry, Bake, Grill & Roast Most Wanted Family Meals

Gaurie Blackburm

Table of Contents

Introduction

The new PowerXL Grill Air Fryer Combo is out now and making a great buzz due to its great capacity and range of cooking options; all other grills have failed to provide so far. The compact size alone is attractive for several customers of this electric grills; with its large capacity, this grill suitable to grill, bake, air fry, roast, slow cook, fry, steam, and reheat meals for all the serving sizes. Indoor grilling is now super easy. All you need is the non-stick grilling grate of the PowerXL grill and adjust it inside the cooker, then select the grilling option and adjust the temperature up to 500 degrees F and grill all sorts of meat, seafood, fruits and veggies. You can close the lid or keep it open to carry out all type of grilling. This cooker is good at providing smokeless cooking. The variety of its cooking programs combined with the temperature adjustment options will amaze you to the core. If you want to know more about this classic PowerXL Product and if you are planning to bring this beauty home, then this cookbook is a perfect read for you, as it has summarized all its features, using a method and suitable recipes in one place. Scroll ahead and find out more.

Chapter 1: The Basics of PowerXL Grill Air Fryer Combo

The PowerXL Grill Air Fryer Combo is a perfect cooker to use in the home kitchen or in a professional setting. Whether you are an expert or a beginner, its range of cooking programs and easy to use control panel will definitely make cooking a convenient job for you. This grill is a breeze for those who want to cook large servings at a time. It is an advanced version of indoor electric Grills since it provides other cooking options as well, and it provides greater capacity and additional cooking functions.

Why Use this Grill?

The following features of the PowerXL Grill make this grill a must to keep cooking appliance:

12 Smart cooking functions:

This grill combines all the cooking functions of an electric cooker, broiler, air fryer, and grill. Imagine you have one single appliance that can carry out all such functions. Each smart program comes with a preset temperature and timer settings, which are also adjustable as per the needs. The 12 cooking programs of the PowerXL Grill include:

- Air Fry
- Grill
- Simmer
- Bake
- Steam
- Roast
- Fry
- Slow Cook
- Sous Vide
- Sauté
- Rice
- Keep Warm

Wide Temperature Range

The best part about this grill is that it comes with a wide range of cooking temperature, which can reduce to as low as 180 degrees F and can be increased to as high as 500 degrees F temperature. This temperature range allows it to carry out all the above-stated functions, from slow cooking to high heat grilling and frying.

- 6 Quart Capacity

The size of the PowerXL Grill takes it to the top of the list when compared to other grills. With its great capacity to accommodate all food types, whether you want to cook chicken pieces, pork chops, salmon fillets inside or want to Air fryer a batch of French fries, the appliance is capable of carrying them all at a time. So, it is perfect to use for families.

- **Easy to Read Display Screen**

The display panel of the PowerXL Grill is easy to understand. It has a display at the center, which is surrounded by the touch keys for all the smart programs, the cooking modes, and the on/off functions. There is a separate button attached to the touch panel, which can be used to adjust the cooking programs, time, and temperature manually.

- **Customizable Programs**

All the smart programs of PowerXL Grill are customizable. Even when the cooking program is running, the settings can be changed using the temperature and time keys and knob. The adjustable programs allow the users to switch from one cooking settings to another with its super flexible heating system.

Even-Heating System

Due to its effective heating mechanism, the PowerXL Grill Air Fryer is capable of heating the food from all sides. This feature ensures even heating. When food is cooked inside this grill, it is cooked well from the top and the bottom.

Auto Shut-Off

Another good feature of this electric cooker is that it has an auto shut system which means that if the machine is left unused after you switch it on then, it will automatically shut off. This feature is great because it saves energy.

Ways to Use this Grill

There are 12 smart programs that give different cooking modes to the users, which are as follow:

- **Air Fry**

Using this program to cook oil-free, crispy food, whether it's coated meat or fries, everything can be fried in its Air fryer basket.

- **Grill**

Indoor grilling is now super easy. All you need is the non-stick grilling grate of the PowerXL grill and adjust it inside the cooker, then select the grilling option and adjust the temperature up to 500-degree F and grill all sorts of meat, seafood, fruits and veggies. You can close the lid or keep it open to carry out all type of grilling. This cooker is good at providing smokeless cooking.

- **Sauté**

There is a sauté mode which is great to carry out open lid cooking. Since sautéing is important in every meal making, this option saves you from using multiple pots for cooking a single meal.

- **Bake**

It is used to bake cakes, brownies, or bread in quick time. Make sure to use a suitable baking dish and a loaf pan for baking these goods in the PowerXL cooker.

- **Steam**

The steam setting provides heat to steam meat, seafood, vegetables and fruits. Steaming can be carried out at various temperatures.

- **Roast**

This cooking program is suitable for roasting meats and vegetables. The powerful lid also assists in roasting the food.

- **Slow Cooker**

The Slow Cook program lets you adjust greater cooking time and lowest temperatures based on the requirements.

- **Keep warm**

Using this mode, the users keep the food warm once it is cooked or even reheat the food, even not served immediately.

- **Sous Vide**

Low-temperature heat is regulated to effectively cook foods in sous vide bags, and the cooker is perfect to create sous vide water bath at these low temperatures. To sous vide your food, you will have to use the tempered glass lid.

Chapter 2: Handling the Grill

When it comes to electric appliances, it is important to inspect all the parts of the appliance before giving it a test run. The PowerXL Grill Air Fryer comes with the following basic elements and accessories.

- The Cooker Base unit
- Non-Stick Inner Pot
- Nonstick grill plate
- Tempered glass lid
- Serving ladle
- Instruction guide
- Recipe book
- Power cord.

The control panel of the appliance is fixed on the front portion of the cooker. The center black panel consists of a touch screen, which shows all the functions. This panel is placed which are used to adjust the time and cooking temperature:

Display: right above the keys, there is a display which lights in white colored figures indicating the time, temperature, and other indicators like Start, Cancel, Lid, Warm, Flip or turn, etc.

Smart Program Keys: The seven smart program keys are located at the bottom of the black panel. Any of the programs can be selected by rotating the preset dial.

Start and Cancel Key: At the bottom of the cooking modes options, there are keys to start or cancel a selected program.

How to Use and Cook

Cooking all sorts of meals in the PowerXL Grill is like a breeze. Following are steps to prepare a fresh and good meal in no time:

- **Prepare the Combo Grill**

Plugin your appliance, and you will the display lighting up instantly. Make sure the appliance is placed over a flat and stable surface. Place the crumb tray inside the cooker at the bottom.

- **Adjust the Required Accessories**

Think about what cooking modes you are going to use, and then select the accessories accordingly. Set the steel racks in any of the three portions to set the food. Use a grilling plate or a cooking pot according to the type and mode of cooking.

- **Preheat If Needed**

To preheat the grill, select the required cooking program and temperature. The preset dial on the left side of the screen is used to switch between the program then adjust the time and temperature after pressing their respective keys and using the dial. Press the start button to initiate preheating.

- **Place the Food Inside**

When the appliance is preheated, the display will indicate that along with a beep. Now you can place the food inside and then close the cooker lid. If you don't want to preheat the appliance, then you can also set the cooking modes, temperature, and time after placing the food. When its food is all set and ready to cook, then you can hit the start button, and it will initiate cooking.

- **Flip and turn the food**

The cooking function is paused when you open the cooker lid and flip the food. Now you can resume the cooking by pressing the start button. The appliance beeps at the end of the cooking program. It's time to serve the food.

After-cooking Cleanup

The PowerXL Grill Air Fryer must be cleaned after every cooking session like any other cooking appliance. It is important to keep the inside of the cooker germs free all the time. The food particles that are stuck at the base or on the walls of the cooker should be cleaned after every session using the following steps:

- Unplug the PowerXL Grill Air Fryer and allow it to cool down completely. Keep the lid open while it cools down.
- Now remove all the grill plate and cooking pot from inside the cooker.
- Place the removable parts of the cooker in the dishwasher and wash them thoroughly.
- Once these accessories are washed, all of them dry out completely.
- Meanwhile, take a clean and slightly damp cloth to clean the inside of the cooker.
- Wipe all the internal walls of the cooker using this cloth. Be gentle while you do the wiping.

- Now use another cloth to clean the exterior of the appliance. Wipe off all the surfaces, especially the touchscreen.
- For cleaning, do not immerse your appliance in the water directly.
- To clean the power plug, use a dry piece of cloth to remove the dirt

Maintenance Tidbits

Your Power XL grill combo is powerful and durable, and you can keep it fresh as new by keeping certain things in mind, such as:

- Keep the appliance closed and prevent any contaminants from entering into its cooking space.
- Avoid placing the appliance anywhere near a heat source, as that may damage its power cord and exterior.
- Avoid placing the appliance where there is even a small chance of water and liquid spills.
- Though the grill grates and cooking plates are non-stick, it advised to grease them with some cooking spray for even cooking and good results.
- Avoid scratching the interior and exterior of the appliance with a hard scrub as that may damage the grill.
- If the display screen shows an error or the timer does not start after pressing the start button, open and close the lid again properly.
- Use the tempered glass lid while slow cooking the food in this cooker.
- Avoid adding items that produce too much foam during cooking.

Chapter 3: Breakfast Recipes

Sweet Potato Porridge

Preparation Time: 10 minutes
Cooking Time: 5 hours
Servings: 6

Ingredients:

- 1 cup fresh apple juice, divided
- 2 pounds sweet potatoes, peeled and cubed into ½-inch size
- 1 tablespoon ground cinnamon
- 1 teaspoon ground nutmeg
- ½ teaspoon ground allspice
- ¼ teaspoons ground cloves
- ¼ cup walnuts, chopped

Method:

1. Plug in the Power XL Grill Air Fryer Combo.
2. In the inner pot, add ½ cup of apple juice and remaining ingredients except for walnuts and mix well.
3. Rotate the "Control Knob" to select "Slow Cook" mode.
4. Press "Timer Button" and rotate the "Control Knob" to set the time for 5 hours.
5. Close the Power XL Grill Air Fryer Combo with "Glass Lid" and press "Start Button" to start cooking.
6. When the cooking time is completed, press "Cancel Button" to stop cooking.
7. Open the lid and stir in the remaining apple juice.
8. With a potato masher, mash the mixture completely.
9. Serve warm with the topping of walnuts.

Nutritional Information per Serving:

- Calories 235
- Total Fat 3.6 g
- Saturated Fat 0.4 g
- Cholesterol 0 mg
- Sodium 16 mg
- Total Carbs 48.6 g
- Fiber 7.4 g
- Sugar 5 g
- Protein 3.7 g

Squash & Apple Porridge

Preparation Time: 10 minutes
Cooking Time: 8 hours
Servings: 8

Ingredients:

- ½ cup raw almonds, soaked for 12 hours and rinsed
- ½ cup raw walnuts, soaked for 12 hours and rinsed
- 2 apples, peeled, cored and cubed
- 1 medium butternut squash, peeled and cubed
- 1 tablespoon applesauce
- 1 teaspoon ground cinnamon
- ¼ teaspoon ground ginger
- ¼ teaspoon ground nutmeg
- 1 cup milk

Method:

1. In a food processor, add nuts and pulse until a meal like texture forms.
2. Plug in the Power XL Grill Air Fryer Combo.
3. In the inner pot, add nut meal and remaining ingredients and gently, stir to combine.
4. Rotate the "Control Knob" to select "Slow Cook" mode.
5. Press "Timer Button" and rotate the "Control Knob" to set the time for 8 hours.
6. Close the Power XL Grill Air Fryer Combo with "Glass Lid" and press "Start Button" to start cooking.
7. When the cooking time is completed, press "Cancel Button" to stop cooking.
8. Open the lid and stir in the remaining apple juice.
9. With a potato masher, mash the mixture slightly.
10. Serve warm.

Nutritional Information per Serving:

- Calories 206
- Total Fat 8.5 g
- Saturated Fat 0.9 g
- Cholesterol 3 mg
- Sodium 22 mg
- Total Carbs 31.6 g
- Fiber 6.2 g
- Sugar 11.5 g
- Protein 6 g

Wheat Berries Porridge

Preparation Time: 10 minutes
Cooking Time: 3 hours
Servings: 4

Ingredients:

- 3 cups water
- 1 cup wheat berries
- Pinch of salt
- 2 cups warm milk
- 2 tablespoons honey
- ½ cup fresh mixed berries

Method:

1. Plug in the Power XL Grill Air Fryer Combo.
2. Fill the inner pot with water.
3. Rotate the "Control Knob" to select "Sous Vide" mode.
4. Press "Timer Button" and rotate the "Control Knob" to set the time for 3 hours.
5. Now press "Temp Button" and rotate the "Control Knob" to set the temperature to 180 degrees F.
6. Close the Power XL Grill Air Fryer Combo with "Glass Lid" and press "Start Button" to preheat.
7. Meanwhile, in a cooking pouch, place the water, wheat berries and salt.
8. Seal the pouch tightly after squeezing out the excess air.
9. When the unit shows "Add Food", open the lid and place the pouch in inner pot.
10. Close the lid and press "Start Button" to start cooking.
11. When the cooking time is completed, press "Cancel Button" to stop cooking.
12. Open the lid and remove the pouch from inner pot.
13. Carefully open the pouch and through a strainer, strain the wheat berries.
14. Divide the wheat berries into 4 serving bowls.
15. Pour milk and drizzle with honey.
16. Top with berries and serve.

Nutritional Information per Serving:

- Calories 156
- Total Fat 2.9 g
- Saturated Fat 1.6 g
- Cholesterol 10 mg
- Sodium 106 mg
- Total Carbs 28.3 g
- Fiber 0.9 g
- Sugar 15.6 g
- Protein 6.2 g

Barley Porridge

Preparation Time: 10 minutes
Cooking Time: 8 hours
Servings: 6

Ingredients:

- 1½ cups pearl barley
- 3 cups unsweetened almond milk
- 3 cups water
- 2 tablespoons maple syrup
- 2 teaspoons fresh orange zest, grated
- 1 teaspoon ground cinnamon
- 1 teaspoon ground ginger
- ¼ teaspoons salt
- ¼ cup walnuts, chopped

Method:

1. Plug in the Power XL Grill Air Fryer Combo.
2. In the inner pot, place all ingredients and stir to combine.
3. Rotate the "Control Knob" to select "Slow Cook" mode.
4. Press "Timer Button" and rotate the "Control Knob" to set the time for 8 hours.
5. Close the Power XL Grill Air Fryer Combo with "Glass Lid" and press "Start Button" to start cooking.
6. When the cooking time is completed, press "Cancel Button" to stop cooking.
7. Open the lid and serve warm.

Nutritional Information per Serving:

- Calories 248
- Total Fat 5.4 g
- Saturated Fat 0.5 g
- Cholesterol 0 mg
- Sodium 196 mg
- Total Carbs 45.5 g
- Fiber 9 g
- Sugar 4.5 g
- Protein 6.8 g

Quinoa Porridge

Preparation Time: 10 minutes
Cooking Time: 1 hour
Servings: 4

Ingredients:

- 1½ cups water
- 1 cup quinoa, rinsed
- Pinch of salt
- 2 cups warm milk
- 2 tablespoons maple syrup
- 1 large banana, peeled and sliced
- 2 tablespoons almonds, chopped

Method:

1. Plug in the Power XL Grill Air Fryer Combo.
2. Fill the inner pot with water.
3. Rotate the "Control Knob" to select "Sous Vide" mode.
4. Press "Timer Button" and rotate the "Control Knob" to set the time for 1 hour.
5. Now press "Temp Button" and rotate the "Control Knob" to set the temperature to 180 degrees F.
6. Close the Power XL Grill Air Fryer Combo with "Glass Lid" and press "Start Button" to preheat.
7. Meanwhile, in a cooking pouch, place the water, quinoa and salt.
8. Seal the pouch tightly after squeezing out the excess air.
9. When the unit shows "Add Food", open the lid and place the pouch in inner pot.
10. Close the lid and press "Start Button" to start cooking.
11. When the cooking time is completed, press "Cancel Button" to stop cooking.
12. Open the lid and remove the pouch from inner pot.
13. Carefully open the pouch and divide the quinoa into 4 serving bowls.
14. Pour milk and drizzle with maple syrup.
15. Top with almonds and serve.

Nutritional Information per Serving:

- Calories 291
- Total Fat 6.7 g
- Saturated Fat 2 g
- Cholesterol 10 mg
- Sodium 100 mg
- Total Carbs 48.4 g
- Fiber 4.2 g
- Sugar 15.6 g
- Protein 11 g

Simple Oatmeal

Preparation Time: 10 minutes
Cooking Time: 3 hours
Servings: 2

Ingredients:

- 2 cups water
- ½ cup steel-cut oats
- Salt, as required
- 2 teaspoons honey
- ¼ cup fresh blueberries

Method:

1. Plug in the Power XL Grill Air Fryer Combo.
2. Fill the inner pot with water.
3. Rotate the "Control Knob" to select "Sous Vide" mode.
4. Press "Timer Button" and rotate the "Control Knob" to set the time for 3 hours.
5. Now press "Temp Button" and rotate the "Control Knob" to set the temperature to 180 degrees F.
6. Close the Power XL Grill Air Fryer Combo with "Glass Lid" and press "Start Button" to preheat.
7. Meanwhile, in a cooking pouch, place the water, oats and salt.
8. Seal the pouch tightly after squeezing out the excess air.
9. When the unit shows "Add Food", open the lid and place the pouch in inner pot.
10. Close the lid and press "Start Button" to start cooking.
11. When the cooking time is completed, press "Cancel Button" to stop cooking.
12. Open the lid and remove the pouch from inner pot.
13. Carefully open the pouch and divide the oats into 2 serving bowls.
14. Top with honey and blueberries and serve.

Nutritional Information per Serving:

- Calories 192
- Total Fat 3.1 g
- Saturated Fat 0 g
- Cholesterol 85 mg
- Sodium 334 mg
- Total Carbs 35.4 g
- Fiber 4.5 g
- Sugar 7.6 g
- Protein 6.2 g

Carrot Oatmeal

Preparation Time: 10 minutes
Cooking Time: 8 hours
Servings: 2

Ingredients:

- ½ cup steel-cut oats
- 1 small carrot, peeled and grated
- 1½ cups milk
- 2 tablespoons unsweetened applesauce
- ¼ teaspoon vanilla extract
- ½ teaspoon ground cinnamon
- Pinch of ground ginger
- Pinch of ground cloves
- Pinch of ground nutmeg

Method:

1. Plug in the Power XL Grill Air Fryer Combo.
2. In the inner pot, place all ingredients and stir to combine.
3. Rotate the "Control Knob" to select "Slow Cook" mode.
4. Press "Timer Button" and rotate the "Control Knob" to set the time for 8 hours.
5. Close the Power XL Grill Air Fryer Combo with "Glass Lid" and press "Start Button" to start cooking.
6. When the cooking time is completed, press "Cancel Button" to stop cooking.
7. Open the lid and serve warm.

Nutritional Information per Serving:

- Calories 273
- Total Fat 6.9 g
- Saturated Fat 2.3 g
- Cholesterol 15 mg
- Sodium 104 mg
- Total Carbs 41 g
- Fiber 5.2 g
- Sugar 11.1 g
- Protein 12.3 g

Oats Granola

Preparation Time: 10 minutes
Cooking Time: 2½ hours
Servings: 16

Ingredients:

- ½ cup sunflower kernels
- 5 cups rolled oats
- 2 tablespoons ground flax seeds
- ¾ cup applesauce
- ¼ cup vegetable oil
- ¼ cup unsalted butter
- 1 teaspoon ground cinnamon
- ½ cup dates, pitted and chopped finely
- ½ cup golden raisins

Method:

1. Plug in the Power XL Grill Air Fryer Combo.
2. In the inner pot, place sunflower kernels, oats, flax seeds, applesauce, oil, butter and cinnamon and stir to combine.
3. Rotate the "Control Knob" to select "Slow Cook" mode.
4. Press "Timer Button" and rotate the "Control Knob" to set the time for 2½ hours, stirring after every 30 minutes.
5. Close the Power XL Grill Air Fryer Combo with "Glass Lid" and press "Start Button" to start cooking.
6. When the cooking time is completed, press "Cancel Button" to stop cooking.
7. Open the lid and transfer the granola into larger baking sheets.
8. Stir in dates and raisins and let it cool completely.

Nutritional Information per Serving:

- Calories 200
- Total Fat 9 g
- Saturated Fat 2.9 g
- Cholesterol 8mg
- Sodium 23 mg
- Total Carbs 27 g
- Fiber 3.8 g
- Sugar 7.7 g
- Protein 4.2 g

Zucchini Omelet

Preparation Time: 10 minutes
Cooking Time: 18 minutes
Servings: 8

Ingredients:

- 10 eggs
- 1 teaspoon fresh basil, chopped
- 1 teaspoon red pepper flakes, crushed
- Salt and ground black pepper, as required
- 4 teaspoons butter
- 4 zucchinis, julienned

Method:

1. In a bowl, add the eggs, basil, red pepper flakes, salt and black pepper and beat until well combined. Set aside.
2. Plug in the Power XL Grill Air Fryer Combo and add the butter in the inner pot.
3. Rotate the "Control Knob" to select "Sauté" mode and press "Start Button" to start cooking.
4. Add the zucchini and cook for about 4-5 minutes, stirring frequently with a wooden spoon.
5. Press "Cancel Button" to stop cooking.
6. Place the egg mixture over zucchini and gently, stir to combine.
7. Rotate the "Control Knob" to select "Air Fry" mode.
8. Press "Timer Button" and rotate the "Control Knob" to set the time for 10 minutes.
9. Now press "Temp Button" and rotate the "Control Knob" to set the temperature to 355 degrees F.
10. Close the Power XL Grill Air Fryer Combo with "Air Frying Lid" and press "Start Button" to start cooking.
11. When the cooking time is completed, press "Cancel Button" to stop cooking.
12. Open the lid and transfer the omelet onto a plate.
13. Cut into equal-sized wedges and serve hot.

Nutritional Information per Serving:

- Calories 112
- Total Fat 7.6 g
- Saturated Fat 3 g
- Cholesterol 210 mg
- Sodium 120 mg
- Total Carbs 3.8 g
- Fiber 1.1 g
- Sugar 2.1g

- Protein 8.2 g

Cheese Omelet

Preparation Time: 10 minutes
Cooking Time: 15 minutes
Servings: 6

Ingredients:

- 12 eggs
- ¾ teaspoons low-sodium soy sauce
- Ground black pepper, as required
- 3 teaspoons butter
- 2 large yellow onions, sliced
- ¾ cup Cheddar cheese, grated

Method:

1. In a bowl, add the eggs, soy sauce and black pepper and beat well. Set aside.
2. Plug in the Power XL Grill Air Fryer Combo and add the butter in the inner pot.
3. Rotate the "Control Knob" to select "Sauté" mode and press "Start Button" to start cooking.
4. Add the onion and cook for about 8-10 minutes, stirring frequently with a wooden spoon.
5. Press "Cancel Button" to stop cooking and place the egg mixture over onion slices, followed by the cheese evenly.
6. Rotate the "Control Knob" to select "Air Fry" mode.
7. Press "Timer Button" and rotate the "Control Knob" to set the time for 5 minutes.
8. Now press "Temp Button" and rotate the "Control Knob" to set the temperature to 355 degrees F.
9. Close the Power XL Grill Air Fryer Combo with "Air Frying Lid" and press "Start Button" to start cooking.
10. When the cooking time is completed, press "Cancel Button" to stop cooking.
11. Open the lid and transfer the omelet onto a plate.
12. Cut into equal-sized wedges and serve hot.

Nutritional Information per Serving:

- Calories 220
- Total Fat 15.4 g
- Saturated Fat 6.9 g
- Cholesterol 347 mg
- Sodium 263 mg
- Total Carbs 5.6 g
- Fiber 1.1 g
- Sugar 2.9 g
- Protein 15.2 g

Bacon & Kale Frittata

Preparation Time: 15 minutes
Cooking Time: 13minutes
Servings: 8

Ingredients:

- 12 eggs
- Salt and ground black pepper, as required
- 1 cup bacon
- 2 tomatoes, cubed
- 1 cup fresh baby kale, chopped
- 1 cup Parmesan cheese, grated

Method:

1. In a small bowl, add the eggs, salt and black pepper and beat well. Set aside.
2. Plug in the Power XL Grill Air Fryer Combo and add the oil in the inner pot.
3. Rotate the "Control Knob" to select "Sauté" mode and press "Start Button" to start cooking.
4. Add the bacon and tomato and cook for about 5 minutes, stirring frequently with a wooden spoon.
5. Add the kale and cook for about 1-2 minutes.
6. Press "Cancel Button" to stop cooking and place the eggs over the pancetta mixture, followed by the cheese.
7. Rotate the "Control Knob" to select "Air Fry" mode.
8. Press "Timer Button" and rotate the "Control Knob" to set the time for 8 minutes.
9. Now press "Temp Button" and rotate the "Control Knob" to set the temperature to 355 degrees F.
10. Close the Power XL Grill Air Fryer Combo with "Air Frying Lid" and press "Start Button" to start cooking.
11. When the cooking time is completed, press "Cancel Button" to stop cooking.
12. Open the lid and transfer the frittata onto a platter.
13. Cut into equal-sized wedges and serve hot.

Nutritional Information per Serving:

- Calories 292
- Total Fat 20.8 g
- Saturated Fat 7.1 g
- Cholesterol 284 mg
- Sodium 853 mg
- Total Carbs 3 g
- Fiber 0.5 g
- Sugar 1.3 g
- Protein 23.2 g

Artichoke Frittata

Preparation Time: 10 minutes
Cooking Time: 3 hours
Servings: 6

Ingredients:

- 8 eggs
- Salt and ground black pepper, as required
- 1 (12-ounce) jar roasted red peppers, drained and chopped
- 1 (14-ounce) can artichoke hearts, drained and chopped
- ¼ cup scallion, chopped
- 4 ounces feta cheese, crumbled

Method:

1. In a bowl, add eggs, salt and black pepper and beat well.
2. Plug in the Power XL Grill Air Fryer Combo.
3. In the inner pot, place the red peppers, artichoke hearts and scallion.
4. Pour egg mixture over vegetables and gently stir to combine.
5. Top with cheese evenly.
6. Rotate the "Control Knob" to select "Slow Cook" mode.
7. Press "Timer Button" and rotate the "Control Knob" to set the time for 3 hours.
8. Close the Power XL Grill Air Fryer Combo with "Glass Lid" and press "Start Button" to start cooking.
9. When the cooking time is completed, press "Cancel Button" to stop cooking.
10. Open the lid and transfer the frittata onto a platter.
11. Cut into equal-sized wedges and serve hot.

Nutritional Information per Serving:

- Calories 181
- Total Fat 10.1 g
- Saturated Fat 4.7 g
- Cholesterol 235 mg
- Sodium 518 mg
- Total Carbs 11.9 g
- Fiber 4.4 g
- Sugar 4.5 g
- Protein 12.8 g

Ham & Veggie Casserole

Preparation Time: 15 minutes
Cooking Time: 1½ hours
Servings: 6

Ingredients:

- 6 large eggs
- ½ cup plain Greek yogurt
- ¼ cup unsweetened coconut milk
- ½ teaspoon dried thyme, crushed
- ½ teaspoon garlic powder
- Salt and ground black pepper, as required
- 1 cup ham, chopped
- 1 cup fresh baby kale, chopped
- 1/3 cup fresh mushrooms, sliced
- 1 cup Pepper Jack cheese, shredded

Method:

1. In a bowl, add eggs, yogurt, milk, thyme, garlic powder, salt and black pepper and beat until smooth.
2. Stir in ham, kale, mushrooms and cheese.
3. Plug in the Power XL Grill Air Fryer Combo.
4. In the inner pot, place the egg mixture.
5. Rotate the "Control Knob" to select "Slow Cook" mode.
6. Press "Timer Button" and rotate the "Control Knob" to set the time for 1½ hours.
7. Close the Power XL Grill Air Fryer Combo with "Glass Lid" and press "Start Button" to start cooking.
8. When the cooking time is completed, press "Cancel Button" to stop cooking.
9. Open the lid and transfer the quiche onto a platter.
10. Cut into equal-sized wedges and serve hot.

Nutritional Information per Serving:

- Calories 220
- Total Fat 14.9 g
- Saturated Fat 7.9 g
- Cholesterol 217 mg
- Sodium 598 mg
- Total Carbs 5.4 g
- Fiber 0.8 g
- Sugar 2.3 g
- Protein 15.9 g

Sausage & Mushroom Casserole

Preparation Time: 15 minutes
Cooking Time: 5 hours 5 minutes
Servings: 8

Ingredients:

- 1 teaspoon butter
- 12 ounces sausage
- 1 cup salsa
- 1 teaspoon red chili powder
- 1 teaspoon ground cumin
- ½ teaspoon ground coriander
- ½ teaspoon garlic powder
- Salt and ground black pepper, as required
- 10 eggs
- 1 cup milk
- 1 cup Cheddar cheese, shredded

Method:

1. Plug in the Power XL Grill Air Fryer Combo and add the butter in the inner pot.
2. Rotate the "Control Knob" to select "Sauté" mode and press "Start Button" to start cooking.
3. Add the sausage and cook for about 4-5 minutes, stirring frequently with a wooden spoon.
4. Press "Cancel Button" to stop cooking and discard the grease from the pot.
5. Transfer the sausage into a bowl and stir in the salsa and spices. Set aside to cool slightly.
6. In a bowl, add the eggs and milk and beat well.
7. Add the sausage mixture and cheese and stir to combine.
8. In the inner pot, place the sausage mixture.
9. Rotate the "Control Knob" to select "Slow Cook" mode.
10. Press "Timer Button" and rotate the "Control Knob" to set the time for 5 hours.
11. Close the Power XL Grill Air Fryer Combo with "Glass Lid" and press "Start Button" to start cooking.
12. When the cooking time is completed, press "Cancel Button" to stop cooking.
13. Open the lid and transfer the casserole onto a platter.
14. Cut into equal-sized wedges and serve hot.

Nutritional Information per Serving:

- Calories 311
- Total Fat 23.5 g
- Saturated Fat 9.3 g
- Cholesterol 259 mg
- Sodium 719 mg
- Total Carbs 4.6 g
- Fiber 0.7 g
- Sugar 2.9 g
- Protein 20.3 g

Eggs with Turkey

Preparation Time: 15 minutes
Cooking Time: 12 minutes
Servings: 6

Ingredients:

- 8 large eggs, divided
- 4 tablespoons heavy cream
- Salt and ground black pepper, as required
- 4 teaspoons unsalted butter, softened
- 4 ounces cooked turkey, sliced thinly
- ¼ teaspoons smoked paprika
- 1/3 cup Parmesan cheese, grated finely
- 4 teaspoons fresh chives, minced

Method:

1. Plug in the Power XL Grill Air Fryer Combo.
2. Rotate the "Control Knob" to select "Air Fry" mode.
3. Press "Timer Button" and rotate the "Control Knob" to set the time for 12 minutes.
4. Now press "Temp Button" and rotate the "Control Knob" to set the temperature to 320 degrees F.
5. Close the Power XL Grill Air Fryer Combo with "Air Frying Lid" and press "Start Button" to preheat.
6. In a bowl, add 2 eggs, cream, salt and black pepper and beat until smooth.
7. When the unit shows "Add Food", open the lid and
8. Spread the butter into the inner pot.
9. Place the turkey slices over the butter and top with the egg mixture evenly.
10. Carefully crack the remaining eggs on top.
11. Sprinkle with paprika, salt and black pepper and top with cheese and chives evenly.
12. Close the lid and press "Start Button" to start cooking.
13. When the cooking time is completed, press "Cancel Button" to stop cooking.
14. Open the lid and serve hot.

Nutritional Information per Serving:

- Calories 201
- Total Fat 14.9 g
- Saturated Fat 6.8 g
- Cholesterol 286 mg
- Sodium 194 mg
- Total Carbs 0.9 g
- Fiber 0.1 g
- Sugar 0.5 g
- Protein 16 g

Chapter 4: Poultry Recipes

Chicken & Strawberry Salad

Preparation Time: 15 minutes
Cooking Time: 1 hour
Servings: 4

Ingredients:

For Chicken Tenders:

- ¼ teaspoons ground cumin
- ¼ teaspoons paprika
- Pinch of ground turmeric
- Salt, as required
- 4 cups chicken tenderloins
- 1 teaspoon olive oil

For Salad:

- 2 cups fresh strawberries, hulled and sliced
- 4 cups fresh baby arugula
- ¼ cup almonds, sliced
- 2 tablespoons olive oil
- 2 tablespoons of fresh lemon juice

Method:

1. Plug in the Power XL Grill Air Fryer Combo.
2. Fill the inner pot with water.
3. Rotate the "Control Knob" to select "Sous Vide" mode.
4. Press "Timer Button" and rotate the "Control Knob" to set the time for 1 hour.
5. Now press "Temp Button" and rotate the "Control Knob" to set the temperature to 140 degrees F.
6. Close the Power XL Grill Air Fryer Combo with "Glass Lid" and press "Start Button" to preheat.
7. Meanwhile, in a bowl, mix together spices and salt.
8. Add chicken tenderloins and coat with spice mixture evenly.
9. In a cooking pouch, place the chicken tenderloins.
10. Seal the pouch tightly after squeezing out the excess air.
11. When the unit shows "Add Food", open the lid and place the pouch in inner pot.
12. Close the lid and press "Start Button" to start cooking.
13. When the cooking time is completed, press "Cancel Button" to stop cooking.
14. Open the lid and remove the pouch from inner pot.
15. Carefully open the pouch and remove the chicken tenderloins.

16. In a skillet, heat oil over medium-high heat and sear the chicken tenderloins for about 1 minute per side.
17. Remove from skillet and set aside to cool slightly.
18. For salad: in a large bowl, add all ingredients and toss to coat well.
19. Top with chicken tenderloins and serve.

Nutritional Information per Serving:

- Calories 287
- Total Fat 8.9 g
- Saturated Fat 1.7 g
- Cholesterol 108 mg
- Sodium 135 mg
- Total Carbs 7.9 g
- Fiber 2.6 g
- Sugar 4.4 g
- Protein 42.9 g

Chicken & Carrot Stew

Preparation Time: 15 minutes
Cooking Time: 6 minutes
Servings: 6

Ingredients:

- 4 (5-ounce) boneless chicken breasts, cubed
- 3 cups carrots, peeled and cubed
- 2 cups celery stalks, chopped
- 1 medium yellow onion, chopped
- 2 garlic cloves, minced
- Salt and ground black pepper, as required
- ½ teaspoon dried thyme
- ½ teaspoon dried rosemary
- 2 cups chicken broth
- 2 tablespoons olive oil

Method:

1. Plug in the Power XL Grill Air Fryer Combo.
2. In the inner pot, add all ingredients except for oil and mix well.
3. Rotate the "Control Knob" to select "Slow Cook" mode.
4. Press "Timer Button" and rotate the "Control Knob" to set the time for 6 hours.
5. Close the Power XL Grill Air Fryer Combo with "Glass Lid" and press "Start Button" to start cooking.
6. When the cooking time is completed, press "Cancel Button" to stop cooking.
7. Open the lid and stir in the oil.
8. Serve hot.

Nutritional Information per Serving:

- Calories 270
- Total Fat 12.3 g
- Saturated Fat 2.8 g
- Cholesterol 84 mg
- Sodium 429 mg
- Total Carbs 8.9 g
- Fiber 2.4 g
- Sugar 4.2 g
- Protein 29.9 g

Herbed Whole Chicken

Preparation Time: 15 minutes
Cooking Time: 1 hour
Servings: 8

Ingredients:

- 1 tablespoon fresh basil, chopped
- 1 tablespoon fresh oregano, chopped
- 1 tablespoon fresh thyme, chopped
- Salt and ground black pepper, as required
- 1 (4½-pounds) whole chicken, necks and giblets removed
- 3 tablespoons olive oil, divided

Method:

1. In a bowl, mix together the herbs, salt and black pepper.
2. Coat the chicken with 2 tablespoons of oil and then, rub inside, outside and underneath the skin with half of the herb mixture generously.
3. Plug in the Power XL Grill Air Fryer Combo.
4. Rotate the "Control Knob" to select "Air Fry" mode.
5. Press "Timer Button" and rotate the "Control Knob" to set the time for 60 minutes.
6. Now press "Temp Button" and rotate the "Control Knob" to set the temperature to 355 degrees F.
7. Close the Power XL Grill Air Fryer Combo with "Air Frying Lid" and press "Start Button" to preheat.
8. When the unit shows "Add Food", open the lid and arrange the chicken, breast-side up into the greased inner pot.
9. Close the lid and press "Start Button" to start cooking.
10. After 30 minutes of cooking, arrange the chicken, breast-side up and oat with the remaining oil.
11. Rub with the remaining herb mixture.
12. When the cooking time is completed, press "Cancel Button" to stop cooking.
13. Open the lid and place the chicken onto a cutting board for about 10 minutes before carving.
14. Cut into desired sized pieces and serve.

Nutritional Information per Serving:

- Calories 533
- Total Fat 24.3 g
- Saturated Fat 6 g
- Cholesterol 227 mg
- Sodium 239 mg
- Total Carbs 0.6 g
- Fiber 0.4 g
- Sugar 0 g

- Protein 73.9 g

Lemony Chicken Legs

Preparation Time: 15 minutes
Cooking Time: 5 hours
Servings: 8

Ingredients:

- 8 skinned chicken drumsticks
- Salt and ground black pepper, as required
- 1 cup unsweetened coconut milk
- 1 thick stalk fresh lemongrass, trimmed and chopped
- 1 (1-inch) fresh ginger piece, chopped
- 4 garlic cloves, minced
- 1 teaspoon five spice powder
- 1 large onion, sliced thinly

Method:

1. Season drumsticks with salt and black pepper.
2. In a blender, add remaining ingredients except for onion and pulse until smooth.
3. In a bowl, add the ginger mixture and chicken and mix well.
4. Plug in the Power XL Grill Air Fryer Combo.
5. In the inner pot, place sliced onion and to with chicken mixture.
6. Rotate the "Control Knob" to select "Slow Cook" mode.
7. Press "Timer Button" and rotate the "Control Knob" to set the time for 5 hours.
8. Close the Power XL Grill Air Fryer Combo with "Glass Lid" and press "Start Button" to start cooking.
9. When the cooking time is completed, press "Cancel Button" to stop cooking.
10. Open the lid and serve hot.

Nutritional Information per Serving:

- Calories 369
- Total Fat 16.9 g
- Saturated Fat 8.9 g
- Cholesterol 150 mg
- Sodium 161 mg
- Total Carbs 4.4 g
- Fiber 1.2 g
- Sugar 1.8 g
- Protein 47.8 g

Gingered Chicken Drumsticks

Preparation Time: 10 minutes
Cooking Time: 25 minutes
Servings: 6

Ingredients:

- ½ cup unsweetened coconut milk
- 4 teaspoons fresh ginger, minced
- 4 teaspoons fresh galangal, minced
- 2 teaspoons ground turmeric
- Salt, as required
- 6 (6-ounce) chicken drumsticks

Method:

1. In a large bowl, place the coconut milk, galangal, ginger, and spices and mix well.
2. Add the chicken drumsticks and coat with the marinade generously.
3. Refrigerate to marinate for at least 6-8 hours.
4. Plug in the Power XL Grill Air Fryer Combo.
5. Rotate the "Control Knob" to select "Air Fry" mode.
6. Press "Timer Button" and rotate the "Control Knob" to set the time for 25 minutes.
7. Now press "Temp Button" and rotate the "Control Knob" to set the temperature to 375 degrees F.
8. Close the Power XL Grill Air Fryer Combo with "Air Frying Lid" and press "Start Button" to preheat.
9. When the unit shows "Add Food", open the lid and arrange the chicken drumsticks into the greased inner pot.
10. Close the lid and press "Start Button" to start cooking.
11. When the cooking time is completed, press "Cancel Button" to stop cooking.
12. Open the lid and serve hot.

Nutritional Information per Serving:

- Calories 342
- Total Fat 14.7 g
- Saturated Fat 6.9 g
- Cholesterol 150 mg
- Sodium 167 mg
- Total Carbs 2.9 g
- Fiber 0.8 g
- Sugar 0.8 g
- Protein 47.5 g

Herbed Chicken Thighs

Preparation Time: 15 minutes
Cooking Time: 8¼ hours
Servings: 8

Ingredients:

- 8 chicken thighs
- Salt and ground black pepper, as required
- 2 garlic cloves, minced
- ½ cup dry white wine
- 1 fresh rosemary sprig
- 1 fresh thyme sprig

Method:

1. Plug in the Power XL Grill Air Fryer Combo.
2. Fill the inner pot with water.
3. Rotate the "Control Knob" to select "Sous Vide" mode.
4. Press "Timer Button" and rotate the "Control Knob" to set the time for 8 hours.
5. Now press "Temp Button" and rotate the "Control Knob" to set the temperature to 176 degrees F.
6. Close the Power XL Grill Air Fryer Combo with "Glass Lid" and press "Start Button" to preheat.
7. Meanwhile, season the chicken thighs with salt and pepper evenly.
8. In a cooking pouch, place the chicken thighs.
9. Seal the pouch tightly after squeezing out the excess air.
10. When the unit shows "Add Food", open the lid and place the pouch in inner pot.
11. Close the lid and press "Start Button" to start cooking.
12. When the cooking time is completed, press "Cancel Button" to stop cooking.
13. Open the lid and remove the pouch from inner pot.
14. Carefully open the pouch and remove the chicken thighs from the pouch.
15. Through a strainer, strain the cooking liquid from pouch into a bowl.
16. With paper towels, gently pat dry the chicken thighs.
17. Heat a heavy-bottomed frying pan over medium-high heat and sear the chicken thighs for about 3 minutes per side.
18. In the same pan, sauté the garlic for about 1 minute.
19. Add the wine and scrape any browned bits from the bottom of the pan.
20. Add the cooking liquid and the herb sprigs and stir to combine.
21. Increase the heat to high and simmer for about 5 minutes.
22. Discard the herb sprigs and stir in the salt and pepper.

23. Serve the chicken thighs alongside the sauce.

Nutritional Information per Serving:

- Calories 339
- Total Fat 12.7 g
- Saturated Fat 3.5 g
- Cholesterol 151 mg
- Sodium 167 mg
- Total Carbs 1.2 g
- Fiber 0.4 g
- Sugar 0.1 g
- Protein 49.3 g

Marinated Chicken Thighs

Preparation Time: 10 minutes
Cooking Time: 30 minutes
Servings: 4

Ingredients:

- 4 (6-ounce) bone-in, skin-on chicken thighs
- Salt and ground black pepper, as required
- ½ cup Italian salad dressing
- 1 teaspoon onion powder
- 1 teaspoon garlic powder

Method:

1. Season the chicken thighs with salt and black pepper evenly.
2. In a large bowl, add the chicken thighs and dressing and mix well.
3. Cover the bowl and refrigerate to marinate overnight.
4. Remove the chicken breast from the bowl and place onto a plate.
5. Sprinkle the chicken thighs with onion powder and garlic powder.
6. Plug in the Power XL Grill Air Fryer Combo.
7. Rotate the "Control Knob" to select "Air Fry" mode.
8. Press "Timer Button" and rotate the "Control Knob" to set the time for 30 minutes.
9. Now press "Temp Button" and rotate the "Control Knob" to set the temperature to 360 degrees F.
10. Close the Power XL Grill Air Fryer Combo with "Air Frying Lid" and press "Start Button" to preheat.
11. When the unit shows "Add Food", open the lid and place chicken thighs into the greased inner pot.
12. Close the lid and press "Start Button" to start cooking.
13. After 15 minutes of cooking time, flip the chicken thighs.
14. When the cooking time is completed, press "Cancel Button" to stop cooking.
15. Open the lid and serve hot.

Nutritional Information per Serving:

- Calories 492
- Total Fat 40.3 g
- Saturated Fat 12.8 g
- Cholesterol 186 mg
- Sodium 167mg
- Total Carbs 4.1 g
- Fiber 0.1 g
- Sugar 2.8 g

- Protein 28.9 g

Bacon-Wrapped Chicken Breasts

Preparation Time: 15 minutes
Cooking Time: 20 minutes
Servings: 4

Ingredients:

- 1 tablespoon sugar
- 8 fresh basil leaves
- 2 tablespoons fish sauce
- 2 tablespoons water
- 2 (8-ounce) boneless chicken breasts, cut each breast in half horizontally
- Salt and ground black pepper, as required
- 8 bacon strips
- 1 tablespoon honey

Method:

1. In a small heavy-bottomed pan, add sugar over medium-low heat and cook for about 2-3 minutes or until caramelized, stirring continuously.
2. Add the basil, fish sauce and water and stir to combine well.
3. Remove from heat and transfer into a large bowl.
4. Sprinkle the chicken with salt and black pepper.
5. Add the chicken pieces into the bowl of basil mixture and coat generously.
6. Refrigerate to marinate for about 4-6 hours.
7. Remove from the bowl and wrap each chicken piece with 2 bacon strips.
8. Coat each chicken piece with honey slightly.
9. Plug in the Power XL Grill Air Fryer Combo.
10. Rotate the "Control Knob" to select "Air Fry" mode.
11. Press "Timer Button" and rotate the "Control Knob" to set the time for 20 minutes.
12. Now press "Temp Button" and rotate the "Control Knob" to set the temperature to 365 degrees F.
13. Close the Power XL Grill Air Fryer Combo with "Air Frying Lid" and press "Start Button" to preheat.
14. When the unit shows "Add Food", open the lid and arrange the chicken breasts into the greased inner pot.
15. Close the lid and press "Start Button" to start cooking.
16. When the cooking time is completed, press "Cancel Button" to stop cooking.
17. Open the lid and serve hot.

Nutritional Information per Serving:

- Calories 557
- Total Fat 32.4 g
- Saturated Fat 10.2 g
- Cholesterol 164mg
- Sodium 2000 mg

- Total Carbs 8.5 g
- Fiber 0 g
- Sugar 7.6 g
- Protein 56.4 g

Crusted Chicken Breasts

Preparation Time: 15 minutes
Cooking Time: 12minutes
Servings: 2

Ingredients:

- 2 (6-ounce) chicken breasts
- Salt and ground black pepper, as required
- ¾ cup oats
- 2 tablespoons mustard powder
- 1 tablespoon fresh parsley
- 2 medium eggs

Method:

1. Place the chicken breasts onto a cutting board and with a meat mallet, flatten each into even thickness.
2. Then, cut each breast in half.
3. Sprinkle the chicken pieces with salt and black pepper and set aside.
4. In a blender, add the oats, mustard powder, parsley, salt and black pepper and pulse until a coarse breadcrumb-like mixture is formed.
5. Transfer the oat mixture into a shallow bowl.
6. In another bowl, crack the eggs and beat well.
7. Coat the chicken with oats mixture and then, dip into beaten eggs and again, coat with the oat mixture.
8. Plug in the Power XL Grill Air Fryer Combo.
9. Rotate the "Control Knob" to select "Air Fry" mode.
10. Press "Timer Button" and rotate the "Control Knob" to set the time for 12 minutes.
11. Now press "Temp Button" and rotate the "Control Knob" to set the temperature to 350 degrees F.
12. Close the Power XL Grill Air Fryer Combo with "Air Frying Lid" and press "Start Button" to preheat.
13. When the unit shows "Add Food", open the lid and arrange the chicken breasts into the greased inner pot.
14. Close the lid and press "Start Button" to start cooking.
15. While cooking, flip the chicken breasts once halfway through.
16. When the cooking time is completed, press "Cancel Button" to stop cooking.
17. Open the lid and place the chicken breasts onto a platter for about 5 minutes before serving.

Nutritional Information per Serving:

- Calories 556
- Total Fat 22.2 g
- Saturated Fat 5.3 g
- Cholesterol 315 mg
- Sodium 289 mg

- Total Carbs 25.1 g
- Fiber 4.8 g
- Sugar 1.4 g
- Protein 61.6 g

Chicken with Zucchini Pasta & Asparagus

Preparation Time: 15minutes
Cooking Time: 8½ hours
Servings: 8

Ingredients:

- 2 pounds skinless, boneless chicken breast tenders
- 1 large onion, chopped
- 2 cups asparagus, trimmed and cut into 2-inch pieces
- 1 tablespoon fresh thyme, chopped
- 1 teaspoon garlic powder
- Salt and ground black pepper, as required
- 4 medium zucchinis, spiralized with blade C
- 1 cup sour cream
- 1 cup cheddar cheese, shredded

Method:

1. Plug in the Power XL Grill Air Fryer Combo.
2. In the inner pot, place the chicken, onion, asparagus, thyme, garlic powder, salt and black pepper and stir to combine.
3. Rotate the "Control Knob" to select "Slow Cook" mode.
4. Press "Timer Button" and rotate the "Control Knob" to set the time for 8½ hours.
5. Close the Power XL Grill Air Fryer Combo with "Glass Lid" and press "Start Button" to start cooking.
6. After cooking of 8 hours, open the lid and place the zucchini over chicken, followed by the cheese and cream.
7. When the cooking time is completed, press "Cancel Button" to stop cooking.
8. Open the lid and stir the mixture well.
9. Serve hot.

Nutritional Information per Serving:

- Calories 292
- Total Fat 15 g
- Saturated Fat 8.3 g
- Cholesterol 93 mg
- Sodium 174 mg
- Total Carbs 8.2 g
- Fiber 2.3 g
- Sugar 3.4 g
- Protein 32 g

Chicken with Beans

Preparation Time: 15 minutes
Cooking Time: 8¼ hours
Servings: 4

Ingredients:

- 1 tablespoon olive oil
- 1 onion, chopped
- 2 garlic cloves, minced
- 1 pound chicken breasts
- 1 teaspoon ground cumin
- 1 cup tomatoes, chopped
- 1 (15-ounce) can black beans, rinsed and drained
- 1 cup canned white beans
- ½ teaspoon cayenne pepper
- Salt and ground black pepper, as required
- 1 cup chicken broth

Method:

1. Plug in the Power XL Grill Air Fryer Combo and add the oil in the inner pot.
2. Rotate the "Control Knob" to select "Sauté" mode and press "Start Button" to start cooking.
3. Add the onion and cook for about 5-6 minutes.
4. Add the garlic and cook for about 1 minute.
5. Add chicken and cook for about 3-4 minutes per side or until browned.
6. Press "Cancel Button" to stop cooking and stir in the remaining ingredients.
7. Rotate the "Control Knob" to select "Slow Cook" mode.
8. Press "Timer Button" and rotate the "Control Knob" to set the time for 8 hours.
9. Close the Power XL Grill Air Fryer Combo with "Glass Lid" and press "Start Button" to start cooking.
10. When the cooking time is completed, press "Cancel Button" to stop cooking.
11. Open the lid and with a slotted spoon, transfer the chicken into a bowl.
12. With 2 forks, shred the meat completely.
13. Add shredded chicken into beans mixture and stir to combine.
14. Serve hot.

Nutritional Information per Serving:

- Calories 484
- Total Fat 13.3 g
- Saturated Fat 3.1 g
- Cholesterol 101 mg
- Sodium 358 mg
- Total Carbs 44.5 g
- Fiber 13.7 g
- Sugar 2.8 g
- Protein 49.1 g

Glazed Turkey Breast

Preparation Time: 10 minutes
Cooking Time: 55 minutes
Servings: 10

Ingredients:

- 1 (5-pound) boneless turkey breast
- Salt and ground black pepper, as required
- 3 tablespoons honey
- 2 tablespoons Dijon mustard
- 1 tablespoon butter, softened

Method:

1. Season the turkey breast with salt and black pepper generously and spray with cooking spray.
2. Plug in the Power XL Grill Air Fryer Combo.
3. Rotate the "Control Knob" to select "Air Fry" mode.
4. Press "Timer Button" and rotate the "Control Knob" to set the time for 55 minutes.
5. Now press "Temp Button" and rotate the "Control Knob" to set the temperature to 350 degrees F.
6. Close the Power XL Grill Air Fryer Combo with "Air Frying Lid" and press "Start Button" to preheat.
7. When the unit shows "Add Food", open the lid and arrange the turkey breast into the greased inner pot.
8. Close the lid and press "Start Button" to start cooking.
9. Meanwhile, for glaze: in a bowl, mix together the maple syrup, mustard and butter.
10. Flip the turkey breast twice, first after 25 minutes and then after 37 minutes.
11. After 50 minutes of cooking, coat the turkey breast with the glaze.
12. When the cooking time is completed, press "Cancel Button" to stop cooking.
13. Open the lid and place the turkey breast onto a cutting board for about 5 minutes before slicing.
14. Cut into desired sized slices and serve.

Nutritional Information per Serving:

- Calories 252
- Total Fat 2.3 g
- Saturated Fat 0.7 g
- Cholesterol 144 mg
- Sodium 170 mg
- Total Carbs 5.4 g
- Fiber 0.1 g
- Sugar 5.2 g

- Protein 56.4 g

Buttered Turkey Breast

Preparation Time: 10 minutes
Cooking Time: 7 hours
Servings: 8

Ingredients:

- ¼ teaspoon garlic, minced
- 2 teaspoons lemon pepper
- ¼ teaspoon paprika
- Salt and ground black pepper, as required
- 1 (5-6 pound) bone-in turkey breast, washed and pat dried
- 2-3 tablespoons unsalted butter, chopped

Method:

1. In a bowl, mix together garlic and spices.
2. Rub turkey breast with garlic mixture generously.
3. Place butter under the skin of breast.
4. Plug in the Power XL Grill Air Fryer Combo.
5. In the greased inner pot, place the turkey breast.
6. Rotate the "Control Knob" to select "Slow Cook" mode.
7. Press "Timer Button" and rotate the "Control Knob" to set the time for 7 hours.
8. Close the Power XL Grill Air Fryer Combo with "Glass Lid" and press "Start Button" to start cooking.
9. When the cooking time is completed, press "Cancel Button" to stop cooking.
10. Open the lid and transfer turkey breast onto a cutting board for about 10-15 minutes before slicing.
11. Cut into desired sized pieces and serve.

Nutritional Information per Serving:

- Calories 508
- Total Fat 23.2 g
- Saturated Fat 6.9 g
- Cholesterol 185 mg
- Sodium 394 mg
- Total Carbs 0.4 g
- Fiber 0.2 g
- Sugar 0 g
- Protein 60.4 g

Citrus Turkey Legs

Preparation Time: 10 minutes
Cooking Time: 30 minutes
Servings: 2

Ingredients:

- 2 garlic cloves, minced
- 1 tablespoon fresh rosemary, minced
- 1 teaspoon fresh lime zest, finely grated
- 2 tablespoons olive oil
- 1 tablespoon fresh lime juice
- Salt and ground black pepper, as required
- 2 turkey legs

Method:

1. In a large bowl, mix together the garlic, rosemary, lime zest, oil, lime juice, salt, and black pepper.
2. Add the turkey legs and coat with marinade generously.
3. Refrigerate to marinate for about 6-8 hours.
4. Plug in the Power XL Grill Air Fryer Combo.
5. Rotate the "Control Knob" to select "Air Fry" mode.
6. Press "Timer Button" and rotate the "Control Knob" to set the time for 30 minutes.
7. Now press "Temp Button" and rotate the "Control Knob" to set the temperature to 350 degrees F.
8. Close the Power XL Grill Air Fryer Combo with "Air Frying Lid" and press "Start Button" to preheat.
9. When the unit shows "Add Food", open the lid and arrange the turkey legs into the greased inner pot.
10. Close the lid and press "Start Button" to start cooking.
11. When the cooking time is completed, press "Cancel Button" to stop cooking.
12. Open the lid and serve hot.

Nutritional Information per Serving:

- Calories 709
- Total Fat 32.7 g
- Saturated Fat 12.1 g
- Cholesterol 450 mg
- Sodium 597 mg
- Total Carbs 2.3 g
- Fiber 0.7 g
- Sugar 0.1 g
- Protein 97.2 g

Turkey & Beans Chili

Preparation Time: 15 minutes
Cooking Time: 5 hours 10 minutes
Servings: 6

Ingredients:

- 1 tablespoon olive oil
- 1 pound ground turkey
- 1 red bell pepper, seeded and chopped
- 1 red onion, chopped finely
- 2 garlic cloves, minced
- 2 cups tomatoes, chopped finely
- 2 cups canned black beans, drained and rinsed
- 2 cups canned kidney beans, drained and rinsed
- ½ cup tomato paste
- 1 tablespoon red chili powder
- 1¼ teaspoons ground cumin
- 1/3 teaspoon garlic powder
- Salt and ground black pepper, as required
- 1 cup chicken broth

Method:

1. Plug in the Power XL Grill Air Fryer Combo and add the oil in the inner pot.
2. Rotate the "Control Knob" to select "Sauté" mode and press "Start Button" to start cooking.
3. Add the turkey and cook for about 8-9 minutes.
4. Add green pepper, onion and garlic and cook for about 1 minute.
5. Press "Cancel Button" to stop cooking and stir in the remaining ingredients.
6. Rotate the "Control Knob" to select "Slow Cook" mode.
7. Press "Timer Button" and rotate the "Control Knob" to set the time for 5 hours.
8. Close the Power XL Grill Air Fryer Combo with "Glass Lid" and press "Start Button" to start cooking.
9. When the cooking time is completed, press "Cancel Button" to stop cooking.
10. Serve hot.

Nutritional Information per Serving:

- Calories 332
- Total Fat 9.2 g
- Saturated Fat 2.3 g
- Cholesterol 54 mg
- Sodium 471 mg
- Total Carbs 38 g
- Fiber 12.4 g
- Sugar 7.9 g
- Protein 27.4 g

Chapter 5: Beef & Lamb Recipes

Beef Salad

Preparation Time: 15 minutes
Cooking Time: 1 hour 36 minutes
Servings: 3

Ingredients:

For Salad:

- ½ pound flank steak
- Salt and ground black pepper, as required
- 1 tablespoon olive oil
- 3 cups Romaine lettuce, torn

- ½ cup cherry tomatoes, halved
- ¼ cup shallots, shaved
- ½ cup walnuts, toasted and chopped
- ¼ cup blue cheese, crumbled

For Dressing:

- 2 garlic cloves, minced
- 1 teaspoon fresh rosemary, minced
- 3 tablespoons extra-virgin olive oil

- 2 tablespoons red wine vinegar
- Salt and ground black pepper, as required

Method:

1. Plug in the Power XL Grill Air Fryer Combo.
2. Fill the inner pot with water.
3. Rotate the "Control Knob" to select "Sous Vide" mode.
4. Press "Timer Button" and rotate the "Control Knob" to set the time for 1½ hours.
5. Now press "Temp Button" and rotate the "Control Knob" to set the temperature to 131 degrees F.
6. Close the Power XL Grill Air Fryer Combo with "Glass Lid" and press "Start Button" to preheat.
7. Meanwhile, in a cooking pouch, place the flank steak.
8. Seal the pouch tightly after squeezing out the excess air.
9. When the unit shows "Add Food", open the lid and place the pouch in inner pot.
10. Close the lid and press "Start Button" to start cooking.
11. When the cooking time is completed, press "Cancel Button" to stop cooking.
12. Open the lid and remove the pouch from inner pot.
13. Carefully open the pouch and remove the steak from the pouch.
14. With paper towels, pat dry the steak.

15. In a skillet, heat oil on medium-high heat and sear the steak for about 1½ minutes per side.
16. Remove the steak from skillet and set aside to cool.
17. Cut the steak into thin slices.
18. For salad: in a large bowl, mix together steak slices and remaining ingredients.
19. For dressing: in a bowl, add all ingredients and beat until well combined.
20. Pour dressing over salad and toss to coat.
21. Serve immediately.

Nutritional Information per Serving:

- Calories 464
- Total Fat 37.5 g
- Saturated Fat 6 g
- Cholesterol 42 mg
- Sodium 100 mg
- Total Carbs 8.1 g
- Fiber 2.3 g
- Sugar 1.6 g
- Protein 27 g

Beef & Spinach Soup

Preparation Time: 10 minutes
Cooking Time: 6 hours
Servings: 6

Ingredients:

- 2 tablespoons unsalted butter, melted
- 4 cups cooked beef, chopped
- 8 cups fresh spinach, chopped
- 1 large carrot, peeled and chopped
- 1 small onion, chopped finely
- ½ tablespoon garlic, minced
- Salt and ground black pepper, as required
- 6 cups chicken broth

Method:

1. Plug in the Power XL Grill Air Fryer Combo.
2. In the inner pot, add all ingredients and mix well.
3. Rotate the "Control Knob" to select "Slow Cook" mode.
4. Press "Timer Button" and rotate the "Control Knob" to set the time for 6 hours.
5. Close the Power XL Grill Air Fryer Combo with "Glass Lid" and press "Start Button" to start cooking.
6. When the cooking time is completed, press "Cancel Button" to stop cooking.
7. Open the lid and serve hot.

Nutritional Information per Serving:

- Calories 309
- Total Fat 12.6 g
- Saturated Fat 5.8 g
- Cholesterol 114 mg
- Sodium 934 mg
- Total Carbs 4.9 g
- Fiber 1.4 g
- Sugar 2 g
- Protein 41.7 g

Bacon-Wrapped Beef Tenderloin

Preparation Time: 10 minutes
Cooking Time: 12 minutes
Servings: 4

Ingredients:

- 8 bacon strips
- 4 (8-ounce) center-cut beef tenderloin filets
- 2 tablespoons olive oil, divided
- Salt and ground black pepper, as required

Method:

1. Wrap 2 bacon strips around the entire outside of each beef filet.
2. With toothpicks, secure each filet.
3. Coat each wrapped filet with oil and sprinkle with salt and black pepper evenly.
4. Plug in the Power XL Grill Air Fryer Combo.
5. Arrange the grill plate in the inner pot.
6. Rotate the "Control Knob" to select "Grill" mode.
7. Press "Timer Button" and rotate the "Control Knob" to set the time for 12 minutes.
8. Close the Power XL Grill Air Fryer Combo with "Air Frying Lid" and press "Start Button" to start preheating.
9. When the unit shows "Add Food", open the lid and arrange the tenderloin filets over the grill plate.
10. Close the lid and press "Start Button" to start cooking.
11. When the cooking time is completed, press "Cancel Button" to stop cooking.
12. Open the lid and transfer the filets onto a platter for about 10 minutes before serving.

Nutritional Information per Serving:

- Calories 850
- Total Fat 54.4 g
- Saturated Fat 17.8 g
- Cholesterol 241 mg
- Sodium 1344 mg
- Total Carbs 0.8 g
- Fiber 0 g
- Sugar 0 g
- Protein 84.4 g

Lemony Beef Roast

Preparation Time: 10 minutes
Cooking Time: 8 hours
Servings: 6

Ingredients:

- 2 pounds beef pot roast, trimmed
- 1 onion, sliced
- 2 garlic cloves, minced
- 1 tablespoon fresh rosemary, minced
- ¼ cup fresh lemon juice
- ½ cup beef broth
- 1 teaspoon ground cumin
- Salt and ground black pepper, as required

Method:

1. Plug in the Power XL Grill Air Fryer Combo.
2. In the inner pot, place all ingredients and stir to combine.
3. Rotate the "Control Knob" to select "Slow Cook" mode.
4. Press "Timer Button" and rotate the "Control Knob" to set the time for 8 hours.
5. Close the Power XL Grill Air Fryer Combo with "Glass Lid" and press "Start Button" to start cooking.
6. When the cooking time is completed, press "Cancel Button" to stop cooking.
7. Open the lid and serve hot.

Nutritional Information per Serving:

- Calories 298
- Total Fat 9.8 g
- Saturated Fat 3.8 g
- Cholesterol 135 mg
- Sodium 167 mg
- Total Carbs 2.8 g
- Fiber 0.7 g
- Sugar 1.1 g
- Protein 46.4 g

Beef Roast with Carrots

Preparation Time: 10 minutes
Cooking Time: 8 hours
Servings: 6

Ingredients:

- 1 (2-pound) beef round roast
- 3 large carrots, peeled and chopped
- 1 large yellow onion, sliced thinly
- 1 cup tomato sauce
- 1 teaspoon ground cumin
- ½ teaspoon ground cinnamon
- Salt and ground black pepper, as required

Method:

1. Plug in the Power XL Grill Air Fryer Combo.
2. In the inner pot, add all ingredients and mix well.
3. Rotate the "Control Knob" to select "Slow Cook" mode.
4. Press "Timer Button" and rotate the "Control Knob" to set the time for 6 hours.
5. Close the Power XL Grill Air Fryer Combo with "Glass Lid" and press "Start Button" to start cooking.
6. When the cooking time is completed, press "Cancel Button" to stop cooking.
7. Open the lid and place the roast onto a cutting board for about 10-15 minutes before slicing.
8. Cut into desired-sized slices and serve.

Nutritional Information per Serving:

- Calories 301
- Total Fat 9.3 g
- Saturated Fat 3.3 g
- Cholesterol 105 mg
- Sodium 324 mg
- Total Carbs 8.4 g
- Fiber 2.3 g
- Sugar 4.6 g
- Protein 43.4 g

Crispy Sirloin Steaks

Preparation Time: 10 minutes
Cooking Time: 14 minutes
Servings: 3

Ingredients:

- ½ cup flour
- Salt and ground black pepper, as required
- 2 eggs
- ¾ cup breadcrumbs
- 3 (6-ounce) sirloin steaks, pounded

Method:

1. In a shallow bowl, place the flour, salt and black pepper and mix well.
2. In a second shallow bowl, beat the eggs.
3. In a third shallow bowl, place the breadcrumbs.
4. Coat the steak with flour, then dip into eggs, and finally coat with the panko mixture.
5. Plug in the Power XL Grill Air Fryer Combo.
6. Rotate the "Control Knob" to select "Air Fry" mode.
7. Press "Timer Button" and rotate the "Control Knob" to set the time for 14 minutes.
8. Now press "Temp Button" and rotate the "Control Knob" to set the temperature to 360 degrees F.
9. Close the Power XL Grill Air Fryer Combo with "Air Frying Lid" and press "Start Button" to preheat.
10. When the unit shows "Add Food", open the lid and arrange the sirloin steaks into the greased inner pot.
11. Close the lid and press "Start Button" to start cooking.
12. When the cooking time is completed, press "Cancel Button" to stop cooking.
13. Open the lid and serve hot.

Nutritional Information per Serving:

- Calories 540
- Total Fat 15.2 g
- Saturated Fat 5.3 g
- Cholesterol 261 mg
- Sodium 402 mg
- Total Carbs 35.4 g
- Fiber 1.9 g
- Sugar 2 g
- Protein 61 g

Seasoned Flank Steak

Preparation Time: 10 minutes
Cooking Time: 30 minutes
Servings: 6

Ingredients:

- 2 pounds flank steak
- 2 tablespoons steak seasoning
- Salt and ground black pepper, as required

Method:

1. Rub the steak with steak seasoning evenly and then sprinkle with salt and black pepper.
2. Plug in the Power XL Grill Air Fryer Combo.
3. Rotate the "Control Knob" of Power XL Grill Air Fryer Combo to select "Bake" mode.
4. Press "Timer Button" and rotate the "Control Knob" to set the time for 30 minutes.
5. Now press "Temp Button" and rotate the "Control Knob" to set the temperature to 425 degrees F.
6. Close the Power XL Grill Air Fryer Combo with "Air Frying Lid" and press "Start Button" to preheat.
7. When the unit shows "Add Food", open the lid and arrange the steak into the greased inner pot.
8. Close the lid and press "Start Button" to start cooking.
9. When the cooking time is completed, press "Cancel Button" to stop cooking.
10. Open the lid and place the steak onto a cutting board for about 10-15 minutes before slicing.
11. With a sharp knife, cut the steak into desired size slices and serve.

Nutritional Information per Serving:

- Calories 293
- Total Fat 12.6 g
- Saturated Fat 5.2 g
- Cholesterol 83 mg
- Sodium 114 mg
- Total Carbs 0 g
- Fiber 0 g
- Sugar 0 g
- Protein 42.1 g

Thyme Beef Brisket

Preparation Time: 10 minutes
Cooking Time: 24 hours
Servings: 3

Ingredients:

- 1 pound beef brisket
- 2 carrots, peeled and chopped roughly
- 1 white onion, chopped roughly
- 1 celery stalk, chopped roughly
- 4 fresh thyme sprigs
- 2 tablespoons unsalted butter
- 2 garlic cloves, peeled
- 1 bay leaf
- Salt and ground black pepper, as required
- ½ cup barbecue sauce

Method:

1. Plug in the Power XL Grill Air Fryer Combo.
2. Fill the inner pot with water.
3. Rotate the "Control Knob" to select "Sous Vide" mode.
4. Press "Timer Button" and rotate the "Control Knob" to set the time for 24 hours.
5. Now press "Temp Button" and rotate the "Control Knob" to set the temperature to 185 degrees F.
6. Close the Power XL Grill Air Fryer Combo with "Glass Lid" and press "Start Button" to preheat.
7. Meanwhile, in a cooking pouch, place all ingredients except for barbecue sauce.
8. Seal the pouch tightly after squeezing out the excess air.
9. When unit shows "Add Food", open the lid and place the pouch in inner pot.
10. Close the lid and press "Start Button" to start cooking.
11. When the cooking time is completed, press "Cancel Button" to stop cooking.
12. Open the lid and remove the pouch from inner pot.
13. Carefully open the pouch and remove the brisket from the pouch.
14. With paper towels, pat dry the brisket.
15. Transfer the brisket onto a cutting board for about 5-10 minutes.
16. Cut into desired slices and serve alongside the barbecue sauce.

Nutritional Information per Serving:

- Calories 335
- Total Fat 13 g
- Saturated Fat 6.3 g
- Cholesterol 117 mg
- Sodium 534 mg
- Total Carbs 17.5 g
- Fiber 1.6 g
- Sugar 10.6 g
- Protein 35.1 g

Lamb Stew

Preparation Time: 15 minutes
Cooking Time: 8 hours
Servings: 6

Ingredients:

- 2 pounds lamb stew meat, cubed
- 2 cups fresh mushrooms, sliced
- 4 garlic cloves, minced
- 1 cup fresh parsley leaves, chopped
- 2 cups tomato paste
- 2 cups beef broth
- Salt and ground black pepper, as required

Method:

1. Plug in the Power XL Grill Air Fryer Combo.
2. In the inner pot, add all ingredients and mix well.
3. Rotate the "Control Knob" to select "Slow Cook" mode.
4. Press "Timer Button" and rotate the "Control Knob" to set the time for 8 hours.
5. Close the Power XL Grill Air Fryer Combo with "Glass Lid" and press "Start Button" to start cooking.
6. When the cooking time is completed, press "Cancel Button" to stop cooking.
7. Open the lid and stir the mixture well.
8. Serve hot.

Nutritional Information per Serving:

- Calories 377
- Total Fat 12.1 g
- Saturated Fat 4.2 g
- Cholesterol 136 mg
- Sodium 489 mg
- Total Carbs 18.9 g
- Fiber 4.2 g
- Sugar 11.6 g
- Protein 49 g

Sweet & Sour Lamb Chops

Preparation Time: 15 minutes
Cooking Time: 40 minutes
Servings: 3

Ingredients:

- 3 (8-ounce) lamb shoulder chops
- Salt and ground black pepper, as required
- ¼ cup brown sugar
- ¼ teaspoon red pepper flakes, crushed
- 2 tablespoons balsamic vinegar

Method:

1. Season the lamb chops with salt and black pepper generously.
2. In a baking pan, place the chops and sprinkle with sugar and red pepper flakes.
3. Drizzle with vinegar.
4. Plug in the Power XL Grill Air Fryer Combo.
5. Rotate the "Control Knob" of Power XL Grill Air Fryer Combo to select "Bake" mode.
6. Press "Timer Button" and rotate the "Control Knob" to set the time for 40 minutes.
7. Now press "Temp Button" and rotate the "Control Knob" to set the temperature to 380 degrees F.
8. Close the Power XL Grill Air Fryer Combo with "Air Frying Lid" and press "Start Button" to preheat.
9. When the unit shows "Add Food", open the lid and arrange the chops into the greased inner pot.
10. Close the lid and press "Start Button" to start cooking.
11. Flip the chops once halfway through.
12. When the cooking time is completed, press "Cancel Button" to stop cooking.
13. Serve hot.

Nutritional Information per Serving:

- Calories 390
- Total Fat 18.1g
- Saturated Fat 6 g
- Cholesterol 151 mg
- Sodium 215 mg
- Total Carbs 12 g
- Fiber 6.7 g
- Sugar 11.8 g
- Protein 44.2 g

Crusted Lamb Chops

Preparation Time: 10 minutes
Cooking Time: 35 minutes
Servings: 6

Ingredients:

- 1¾ pounds rack of lamb
- Salt and ground black pepper, as required
- 1 egg
- 1 tablespoon breadcrumbs
- 3 ounces pistachios, chopped finely

Method:

1. Season the rack of lamb with salt and black pepper evenly and then drizzle with cooking spray.
2. In a shallow dish, beat the egg.
3. In another shallow dish, mix together the breadcrumbs and pistachios.
4. Dip the rack of lamb in egg and then coat with the pistachio mixture.
5. Plug in the Power XL Grill Air Fryer Combo.
6. Rotate the "Control Knob" to select "Air Fry" mode.
7. Press "Timer Button" and rotate the "Control Knob" to set the time for 30 minutes.
8. Now press "Temp Button" and rotate the "Control Knob" to set the temperature to 220 degrees F.
9. Close the Power XL Grill Air Fryer Combo with "Air Frying Lid" and press "Start Button" to preheat.
10. When the unit shows "Add Food", open the lid and arrange the rack into the greased inner pot.
11. Close the lid and press "Start Button" to start cooking.
12. After 30 minutes of cooking, rotate the "Control Knob" to set the temperature to 390 degrees F for 5 minutes.
13. When the cooking time is completed, press "Cancel Button" to stop cooking.
14. Open the lid and place the rack onto a cutting board.
15. Cut the rack into individual chops and serve hot.

Nutritional Information per Serving:

- Calories 313
- Total Fat 19.1 g
- Saturated Fat 5.1 g
- Cholesterol 115 mg
- Sodium 216 mg
- Total Carbs 4.7 g
- Fiber 1.5 g
- Sugar 1.1 g
- Protein 30.8 g

Garlicky Leg of Lamb

Preparation Time: 10 minutes
Cooking Time: 8 hours
Servings: 10

Ingredients:

- 3 pounds boneless leg of lamb, rolled
- 6 garlic cloves, minced
- Salt and ground black pepper, as required
- ½ cup beef broth
- 2-3 tablespoons fresh lemon juice

Method:

1. Plug in the Power XL Grill Air Fryer Combo.
2. In the inner pot, add all the ingredients and mix well.
3. Rotate the "Control Knob" to select "Slow Cook" mode.
4. Press "Timer Button" and rotate the "Control Knob" to set the time for 8 hours.
5. Close the Power XL Grill Air Fryer Combo with "Glass Lid" and press "Start Button" to start cooking.
6. When the cooking time is completed, press "Cancel Button" to stop cooking.
7. Open the lid and place the leg of lamb onto a cutting board for about 10 minutes.
8. Cut the leg of lamb into desired-sized pieces and serve.

Nutritional Information per Serving:

- Calories 258
- Total Fat 10.1 g
- Saturated Fat 3.8 g
- Cholesterol 122 mg
- Sodium 158 mg
- Total Carbs 0.7 g
- Fiber 0.1 g
- Sugar 0.1 g
- Protein 38.4 g

Lamb & Beans Chili

Preparation Time: 15 minutes
Cooking Time: 5 hours 10 minutes
Servings: 6

Ingredients:

- 1¼ pounds lean ground lamb
- 1 green bell pepper, seeded and chopped
- 1 onion, chopped finely
- 1 celery stalk, chopped
- 2 garlic cloves, minced
- 3 cups tomatoes, chopped finely
- 4 cups canned black beans, drained and rinsed
- 1 teaspoon dried thyme
- 1 tablespoon chili powder
- 1 teaspoon ground cumin
- Salt and ground black pepper, as required
- 1 cup chicken broth
- ½ cup fresh cilantro, chopped

Method:

1. Plug in the Power XL Grill Air Fryer Combo and add the oil in the inner pot.
2. Rotate the "Control Knob" to select "Sauté" mode and press "Start Button" to start cooking.
3. Add lamb and cook for about 8-9 minutes.
4. Add bell pepper, onion, celery and garlic and cook for about 1 minute.
5. Press "Cancel Button" to stop cooking and stir in the remaining ingredients.
6. Rotate the "Control Knob" to select "Slow Cook" mode.
7. Press "Timer Button" and rotate the "Control Knob" to set the time for 5 hours.
8. Close the Power XL Grill Air Fryer Combo with "Glass Lid" and press "Start Button" to start cooking.
9. When the cooking time is completed, press "Cancel Button" to stop cooking.
10. Open the lid and serve hot with the topping of cilantro.

Nutritional Information per Serving:

- Calories 345
- Total Fat 7 g
- Saturated Fat 2.3 g
- Cholesterol 68 mg
- Sodium 472 mg
- Total Carbs 38.1 g
- Fiber 12.4 g
- Sugar 7.9 g
- Protein 33.8 g

Chapter 6: Pork Recipes

Pork & Veggie Soup

Preparation Time: 15 minutes
Cooking Time: 8 hours
Servings: 8

Ingredients:

- 6 cups chicken broth, divided
- 1½ pounds cherry tomatoes, halved
- 2 garlic cloves, minced
- 2 tablespoons Italian seasoning
- 1 medium sweet potato, peeled and chopped
- 2 cups carrots, peeled and chopped
- 1 bulb fennel, sliced
- 2 celery stalks, chopped
- 2 pounds boneless pork, cubed
- 1 bay leaf
- Salt and ground black pepper, as required

Method:

1. In a blender, add 2 cups of broth, tomatoes, garlic and seasoning and pulse until smooth.
2. Plug in the Power XL Grill Air Fryer Combo.
3. In the inner pot, place the vegetables.
4. Place pork over vegetables.
5. Now, add tomato sauce and remaining broth.
6. Rotate the "Control Knob" to select "Slow Cook" mode.
7. Press "Timer Button" and rotate the "Control Knob" to set the time for 8 hours.
8. Close the Power XL Grill Air Fryer Combo with "Glass Lid" and press "Start Button" to start cooking.
9. When the cooking time is completed, press "Cancel Button" to stop cooking.
10. Open the lid and serve hot.

Nutritional Information per Serving:

- Calories 251
- Total Fat 6.3 g
- Saturated Fat 1.8 g
- Cholesterol 85 mg
- Sodium 704 mg
- Total Carbs 12.3 g
- Fiber 3.2 g
- Sugar 5.4 g
- Protein 35 g

Pork & Rutabaga Stew

Preparation Time: 15 minutes
Cooking Time: 8 hours
Servings: 8

Ingredients:

- 2½ pounds boneless country style pork ribs
- 2 cups rutabaga, peeled and cubed
- 2 cups tomatoes, chopped finely
- ½ cup onion, chopped
- 2 garlic cloves, minced
- 2 tablespoons unsalted butter
- 4 cups chicken broth
- 1 tablespoon fresh oregano, minced
- Salt and ground black pepper, as required

Method:

1. Plug in the Power XL Grill Air Fryer Combo.
2. In the inner pot, add all the ingredients and stir to combine.
3. Rotate the "Control Knob" to select "Slow Cook" mode.
4. Press "Timer Button" and rotate the "Control Knob" to set the time for 8 hours.
5. Close the Power XL Grill Air Fryer Combo with "Glass Lid" and press "Start Button" to start cooking.
6. After 7½ hours of cooking, open the lid and with a slotted spoon, transfer the pork onto large plate.
7. With 2 forks, shred the pork completely.
8. Return the shredded pork into the inner pot and stir to combine.
9. When the cooking time is completed, press "Cancel Button" to stop cooking.
10. Open the lid and serve hot.

Nutritional Information per Serving:

- Calories 275
- Total Fat 8.8 g
- Saturated Fat 3.7 g
- Cholesterol 111 mg
- Sodium 512 mg
- Total Carbs 6.3 g
- Fiber 1.8 g
- Sugar 3.8 g
- Protein 40.4 g

Pineapple Pulled Pork

Preparation Time: 10 minutes
Cooking Time: 6 hours
Servings: 10

Ingredients:

- 3 pounds pork shoulder
- 1 small can crushed pineapple with liquids
- 2 tablespoons fresh ginger, grated

Method:

1. Plug in the Power XL Grill Air Fryer Combo.
2. In the inner pot, add all the ingredients and stir to combine.
3. Rotate the "Control Knob" to select "Slow Cook" mode.
4. Press "Timer Button" and rotate the "Control Knob" to set the time for 8 hours.
5. Close the Power XL Grill Air Fryer Combo with "Glass Lid" and press "Start Button" to start cooking.
6. When the cooking time is completed, press "Cancel Button" to stop cooking.
7. Open the lid and with 2 forks, shred the pork completely.
8. Serve hot.

Nutritional Information per Serving:

- Calories 415
- Total Fat 29.2 g
- Saturated Fat 10.7 g
- Cholesterol 122 mg
- Sodium 162 mg
- Total Carbs 4.5 g
- Fiber 0.5 g
- Sugar 2.8 g
- Protein 31.9 g

Spicy Pork Roast

Preparation Time: 10 minutes
Cooking Time: 8 hours
Servings: 12

Ingredients:

- 1 teaspoon dried rosemary, crushed
- 1 teaspoon dried thyme, crushed
- 1 teaspoon cayenne pepper
- ½ teaspoon smoked paprika
- Salt and ground black pepper, as required
- 4 pounds boneless pork roast
- 1 medium white onion, sliced thinly and divided
- 1 cup hot chicken broth

Method:

1. Plug in the Power XL Grill Air Fryer Combo.
2. In the inner pot, add all the ingredients and stir to combine.
3. Rotate the "Control Knob" to select "Slow Cook" mode.
4. Press "Timer Button" and rotate the "Control Knob" to set the time for 8 hours.
5. Close the Power XL Grill Air Fryer Combo with "Glass Lid" and press "Start Button" to start cooking.
6. When the cooking time is completed, press "Cancel Button" to stop cooking.
7. Open the lid and with 2 forks, shred the pork completely.
8. Serve hot.

Nutritional Information per Serving:

- Calories 225
- Total Fat 5.5 g
- Saturated Fat 1.9 g
- Cholesterol 110 mg
- Sodium 162 mg
- Total Carbs 1.2 g
- Fiber 0.3 g
- Sugar 0.5 g
- Protein 40.1 g

Seasoned Pork Loin

Preparation Time: 10 minutes
Cooking Time: 30 minutes
Servings: 6

Ingredients:

- 2 pounds pork loin
- 2 tablespoons olive oil, divided
- 2-3 tablespoons pork rub seasoning

Method:

1. Coat the pork loin with oil and then, rub with seasoning.
2. Plug in the Power XL Grill Air Fryer Combo.
3. Rotate the "Control Knob" to select "Bake" mode.
4. Press "Timer Button" and rotate the "Control Knob" to set the time for 30 minutes.
5. Now press "Temp Button" and rotate the "Control Knob" to set the temperature to 350 degrees F.
6. Close the Power XL Grill Air Fryer Combo with "Air Frying Lid" and press "Start Button" to preheat.
7. When unit shows "Add Food", open the lid and arrange the pork loin into the greased inner pot.
8. Close the lid and press "Start Button" to start cooking.
9. When the cooking time is completed, press "Cancel Button" to stop cooking.
10. Open the lid and place the pork loin onto a cutting board.
11. With a piece of foil, cover the pork loin for about 10 minutes before slicing.
12. With a sharp knife, cut the pork loin into desired size slices and serve.

Nutritional Information per Serving:

- Calories 412
- Total Fat 25.6 g
- Saturated Fat 8.6 g
- Cholesterol 121 mg
- Sodium 234 mg
- Total Carbs 2 g
- Fiber 0 g
- Sugar 0 g
- Protein 41.4 g

Rosemary Pork Loin

Preparation Time: 10 minutes
Cooking Time: 20 minutes
Servings: 6

Ingredients:

- 3 tablespoons sugar
- 2 teaspoons dried rosemary
- 1 teaspoon garlic powder
- Salt, as required
- 2 pounds pork loin

Method:

1. In a bowl, add the sugar, rosemary, garlic powder and salt and mix well.
2. Rub the pork loin with bail mixture generously.
3. Plug in the Power XL Grill Air Fryer Combo.
4. Rotate the "Control Knob" to select "Air Fry" mode.
5. Press "Timer Button" and rotate the "Control Knob" to set the time for 20 minutes.
6. Now press "Temp Button" and rotate the "Control Knob" to set the temperature to 400 degrees F.
7. Close the Power XL Grill Air Fryer Combo with "Air Frying Lid" and press "Start Button" to preheat.
8. When the unit shows "Add Food", open the lid and arrange the pork loin into the greased inner pot.
9. Close the lid and press "Start Button" to start cooking.
10. Flip the loin once halfway through.
11. When the cooking time is completed, press "Cancel Button" to stop cooking.
12. Open the lid and place the pork loin onto a cutting board.
13. Cut into desired-sized slices and serve.

Nutritional Information per Serving:

- Calories 391
- Total Fat 21.9 g
- Saturated Fat 7.8 g
- Cholesterol 121 mg
- Sodium 121 mg
- Total Carbs 6.6 g
- Fiber 0.2 g
- Sugar 6.1 g
- Protein 41.4 g

Glazed Pork Tenderloin

Preparation Time: 15 minutes
Cooking Time: 20 minutes
Servings: 3

Ingredients:

- 2 tablespoons red hot sauce
- 2 tablespoons maple syrup
- 1 tablespoon fresh thyme, minced
- ¼ teaspoon red pepper flakes, crushed
- Salt, as required
- 1 pound pork tenderloin

Method:

1. In a small bowl, add the hot sauce, maple syrup, thyme, red pepper flakes and salt and mix well.
2. Brush the pork tenderloin with mixture evenly.
3. Plug in the Power XL Grill Air Fryer Combo.
4. Rotate the "Control Knob" to select "Air Fry" mode.
5. Press "Timer Button" and rotate the "Control Knob" to set the time for 20 minutes.
6. Now press "Temp Button" and rotate the "Control Knob" to set the temperature to 350 degrees F.
7. Close the Power XL Grill Air Fryer Combo with "Air Frying Lid" and press "Start Button" to preheat.
8. When unit shows "Add Food", open the lid and arrange the pork tenderloin into the greased inner pot.
9. Close the lid and press "Start Button" to start cooking.
10. When the cooking time is completed, press "Cancel Button" to stop cooking.
11. Open the lid and place the pork tenderloin onto a cutting board for about 10 minutes before slicing.
12. With a sharp knife, cut the tenderloin into desired sized slices and serve.

Nutritional Information per Serving:

- Calories 255
- Total Fat 5.5 g
- Saturated Fat 1.8 g
- Cholesterol 110 mg
- Sodium 394 mg
- Total Carbs 9.8 g
- Fiber 04 g
- Sugar 8.1 g
- Protein 39.7 g

Herbs & Mustard Pork Chops

Preparation Time: 10 minutes
Cooking Time: 12 minutes
Servings: 2

Ingredients:

- 2 garlic cloves, minced
- ½ tablespoon fresh cilantro, chopped
- ½ tablespoon fresh rosemary, chopped
- ½ tablespoon fresh parsley, chopped
- 2 tablespoons olive oil
- ¾ tablespoons Dijon mustard
- 1 tablespoon ground coriander
- 1 teaspoon sugar
- Salt, as required
- 2 (6-ounce) (1-inch thick) pork chops

Method:

1. In a bowl, mix together the garlic, herbs, oil, mustard, coriander, sugar, and salt.
2. Add the pork chops and coat with marinade generously.
3. Cover and refrigerate for about 2-3 hours.
4. Remove the chops from the refrigerator and set aside at room temperature for about 30 minutes.
5. Plug in the Power XL Grill Air Fryer Combo.
6. Rotate the "Control Knob" to select "Air Fry" mode.
7. Press "Timer Button" and rotate the "Control Knob" to set the time for 12 minutes.
8. Now press "Temp Button" and rotate the "Control Knob" to set the temperature to 390 degrees F.
9. Close the Power XL Grill Air Fryer Combo with "Air Frying Lid" and press "Start Button" to preheat.
10. When the unit shows "Add Food", open the lid and arrange the pork chops into the greased inner pot.
11. Close the lid and press "Start Button" to start cooking.
12. When the cooking time is completed, press "Cancel Button" to stop cooking.
13. Open the lid and serve hot.

Nutritional Information per Serving:

- Calories 683
- Total Fat 56.7 g
- Saturated Fat 17.9 g
- Cholesterol 145 mg
- Sodium 265 mg
- Total Carbs 3.9 g
- Fiber 0.6 g
- Sugar 2.1 g

- Protein 38.8 g

Citrus Pork Chops

Preparation Time: 10 minutes
Cooking Time: 15 minutes
Servings: 4

Ingredients:

- ¼ cup extra-virgin olive oil
- ½ cup fresh orange juice
- ¼ cup fresh lime juice
- ½ cup fresh cilantro, chopped finely
- ¼ cup fresh mint leaves, chopped finely
- 4 garlic cloves, minced
- 1 tablespoon orange zest, grated
- 1 teaspoon lime zest, grated
- 1 teaspoon dried oregano
- 1 teaspoon ground cumin
- Salt and ground black pepper, as required
- 4 thick-cut pork chops

Method:

1. In a bowl, add all ingredients and mix well.
2. Cover the bowl and refrigerate to marinate overnight.
3. Remove the pork chops from the bowl of marinade and drip off the excess marinade.
4. Plug in the Power XL Grill Air Fryer Combo.
5. Arrange the grill plate in the inner pot.
6. Rotate the "Control Knob" to select "Grill" mode.
7. Press "Timer Button" and rotate the "Control Knob" to set the time for 15 minutes.
8. Close the Power XL Grill Air Fryer Combo with "Air Frying Lid" and press "Start Button" to start preheating.
9. When the unit shows "Add Food", open the lid and arrange the pork chops over the grill plate.
10. When the cooking time is completed, press "Cancel Button" to stop cooking.
11. Open the lid and serve hot.

Nutritional Information per Serving:

- Calories 680
- Total Fat 55.2 g
- Saturated Fat 17.7 g
- Cholesterol 145 mg
- Sodium 162 mg
- Total Carbs 5.8 g
- Fiber 1 g
- Sugar 2.7 g
- Protein 39 g

Braised Pork Ribs

Preparation Time: 10 minutes
Cooking Time: 10 hours
Servings: 6

Ingredients:

- 3 pounds pork ribs
- 1 small onion, chopped
- 2 garlic cloves, minced
- 1 cup baby carrots, peeled and chopped
- ½ cup chicken broth
- ¼ cup low-sodium soy sauce
- 1 tablespoon olive oil
- Ground black pepper, as required

Method:

1. Plug in the Power XL Grill Air Fryer Combo.
2. In the inner pot, add all ingredients and mix well.
3. Rotate the "Control Knob" to select "Slow Cook" mode.
4. Press "Timer Button" and rotate the "Control Knob" to set the time for 10 hours.
5. Close the Power XL Grill Air Fryer Combo with "Glass Lid" and press "Start Button" to start cooking.
6. When the cooking time is completed, press "Cancel Button" to stop cooking.
7. Open the lid and serve hot.

Nutritional Information per Serving:

- Calories 506
- Total Fat 32 g
- Saturated Fat 13.1 g
- Cholesterol 175 mg
- Sodium 195 mg
- Total Carbs 5.8 g
- Fiber 1.8 g
- Sugar 3.1 g
- Protein 46.4 g

BBQ Pork Spare Ribs

Preparation Time: 10 minutes
Cooking Time: 26 minutes
Servings: 4

Ingredients:

- ¼ cup maple syrup, divided
- ¾ cup apple BBQ sauce
- 2 tablespoons tomato ketchup
- 1 tablespoon Worcestershire sauce
- 1 tablespoon low-sodium soy sauce
- Freshly ground white pepper, as required
- 1¾ pounds pork ribs

Method:

1. In a bowl, mix together 3 tablespoons of maple syrup and the remaining ingredients except pork ribs.
2. Add the pork ribs and coat with the mixture generously.
3. Refrigerate to marinate for about 20 minutes.
4. Plug in the Power XL Grill Air Fryer Combo.
5. Rotate the "Control Knob" to select "Air Fry" mode.
6. Press "Timer Button" and rotate the "Control Knob" to set the time for 26 minutes.
7. Now press "Temp Button" and rotate the "Control Knob" to set the temperature to 355 degrees F.
8. Close the Power XL Grill Air Fryer Combo with "Air Frying Lid" and press "Start Button" to preheat.
9. When unit shows "Add Food", open the lid and arrange the pork ribs into the greased inner pot.
10. Close the lid and press "Start Button" to start cooking.
11. Flip the ribs once halfway through.
12. When the cooking time is completed, press "Cancel Button" to stop cooking.
13. Open the lid and transfer the ribs onto serving plates.
14. Drizzle with the remaining maple syrup and serve immediately.

Nutritional Information per Serving:

- Calories 783
- Total Fat 47.7 g
- Saturated Fat 19.8 g
- Cholesterol 145 mg
- Sodium 1334 mg
- Total Carbs 34.4 g
- Fiber 0 g
- Sugar 31.2 g

- Protein 52 g

Pork Sausage & Oats Pilaf

Preparation Time: 10 minutes
Cooking Time: 9 hours
Servings: 6

Ingredients:

- 1 tablespoon unsalted butter
- 1 pound pork sausage
- 2 cups steel-cut oats
- 8½ cups chicken broth
- Pinch of garlic powder
- Salt and ground black pepper, as required

Method:

1. Plug in the Power XL Grill Air Fryer Combo and add the butter in the inner pot.
2. Rotate the "Control Knob" to select "Sauté" mode and press "Start Button" to start cooking.
3. Add the sausage and cook for about 10 minutes or until browned.
4. Press "Cancel Button" to stop cooking and transfer the sausage onto a plate.
5. Cut each sausage into ½-inch slices.
6. In the inner pot, place the sausage slices and remaining ingredients and stir to combine.
7. Rotate the "Control Knob" to select "Slow Cook" mode.
8. Press "Timer Button" and rotate the "Control Knob" to set the time for 9 hours.
9. Close the Power XL Grill Air Fryer Combo with "Glass Lid" and press "Start Button" to start cooking.
10. When the cooking time is completed, press "Cancel Button" to stop cooking.
11. Open the lid and serve hot.

Nutritional Information per Serving:

- Calories 541
- Total Fat 29.3 g
- Saturated Fat 8.7 g
- Cholesterol 69 mg
- Sodium 1234 mg
- Total Carbs 37.4 g
- Fiber 5.3 g
- Sugar 1 g
- Protein 29.6 g

Pork with Apple

Preparation Time: 10 minutes
Cooking Time: 6 hours
Servings: 8

Ingredients:

- 4 apples, cored and sliced
- 2 pounds pork tenderloin, trimmed
- 1 teaspoon ground nutmeg
- 2 tablespoons soy sauce

Method:

1. With a sharp knife, make slits into the pork.
2. Plug in the Power XL Grill Air Fryer Combo.
3. In the inner pot, place half of apple slices and arrange the pork tenderloin on top.
4. Sprinkle with half of nutmeg.
5. Place the remaining apple slices over pork tenderloin and sprinkle with remaining nutmeg.
6. Pour the soy sauce on top.
7. Rotate the "Control Knob" to select "Slow Cook" mode.
8. Press "Timer Button" and rotate the "Control Knob" to set the time for 6 hours.
9. Close the Power XL Grill Air Fryer Combo with "Glass Lid" and press "Start Button" to start cooking.
10. When the cooking time is completed, press "Cancel Button" to stop cooking.
11. Open the lid and serve hot.

Nutritional Information per Serving:

- Calories 224
- Total Fat 4.3 g
- Saturated Fat 1.4 g
- Cholesterol 83 mg
- Sodium 291 mg
- Total Carbs 15.8 g
- Fiber 2.8 g
- Sugar 11.8 g
- Protein 30.3 g

Pork Meatballs in Tomato Gravy

Preparation Time: 15 minutes
Cooking Time: 4 hours
Servings: 6

Ingredients:

For Meatballs:

- 1 pound lean ground pork
- 1 pound pork sausage, casing removed and crumbled
- 1 egg, beaten
- ¼ cup Parmesan cheese, grated
- 1/3 cup whole-wheat breadcrumbs
- 1 tablespoons fresh basil leaves, chopped
- 1 tablespoons fresh parsley, chopped
- ½ teaspoon garlic powder
- Salt and ground black pepper, as required

For Gravy:

- 3 (14½-ounce) cans crushed tomatoes with liquid
- 2 tablespoons fresh basil leaves, chopped
- 2 tablespoons fresh parsley, chopped
- 1 teaspoon garlic powder
- 1 teaspoon cayenne pepper
- Salt and ground black pepper, as required

Method:

1. For meatballs: in a large bowl, add all ingredients and mix until well combined.
2. Make equal-sized small balls from mixture.
3. Plug in the Power XL Grill Air Fryer Combo.
4. In the inner pot, add all gravy ingredients and stir to combine.
5. Place the meatballs and gently submerge in the gravy.
6. Rotate the "Control Knob" to select "Slow Cook" mode.
7. Press "Timer Button" and rotate the "Control Knob" to set the time for 4 hours.
8. Close the Power XL Grill Air Fryer Combo with "Glass Lid" and press "Start Button" to start cooking.
9. When the cooking time is completed, press "Cancel Button" to stop cooking.
10. Open the lid and serve hot.

Nutritional Information per Serving:

- Calories 540
- Total Fat 34.7 g
- Saturated Fat 7.6 g
- Cholesterol 93 mg
- Sodium 934 mg
- Total Carbs 21.2 g
- Fiber 7 g
- Sugar 12 g
- Protein 35.7 g

Pork & Bacon Chili

Preparation Time: 15 minutes
Cooking Time: 6 hours 10 minutes
Servings: 8

Ingredients:

- 2 medium green bell peppers, seeded and chopped
- 1 medium onion, chopped
- ½ tablespoon olive oil
- 2 pounds lean ground pork
- Freshly ground black pepper, as required
- 8 thick bacon slices, chopped
- 2 cups tomatoes, chopped
- 1½ teaspoons ground cumin
- 2 teaspoons red chili powder
- ½ teaspoon cayenne pepper
- ¾ cup tomato paste
- ¼ cup chicken broth
- ¼ cup cheddar cheese, shredded

Method:

1. Plug in the Power XL Grill Air Fryer Combo and add the oil in the inner pot.
2. Rotate the "Control Knob" to select "Sauté" mode and press "Start Button" to start cooking.
3. Add the pork with salt and black pepper and cook for about 4-5 minutes, stirring frequently with a wooden spoon.
4. Transfer the pork into a bowl.
5. In the pot, add the bacon and cook for 4-5 minutes.
6. Press "Cancel Button" to stop cooking and transfer the bacon onto a palate.
7. In the bottom of pot, place the bell pepper and onion.
8. Place the pork over onion mixture, followed by the cooked bacon and tomatoes.
9. Sprinkle with spices evenly and top with tomato paste and broth.
10. Rotate the "Control Knob" to select "Slow Cook" mode.
11. Press "Timer Button" and rotate the "Control Knob" to set the time for 6 hours.
12. Close the Power XL Grill Air Fryer Combo with "Glass Lid" and press "Start Button" to start cooking.
13. When the cooking time is completed, press "Cancel Button" to stop cooking.
14. Open the lid and serve hot with the topping of cheddar.

Nutritional Information per Serving:

- Calories 456
- Total Fat 31.6 g
- Saturated Fat 4.9 g
- Cholesterol 35 mg
- Sodium 745 mg
- Total Carbs 11 g
- Fiber 2.5 g
- Sugar 6.4 g
- Protein 33 g

Chapter 7: Seafood Recipes

Trout Salad

Preparation Time: 15 minutes
Cooking Time: 15 minutes
Servings: 3

Ingredients:

For Trout:

- 2 (4-ounce) skinless trout fillets, sliced into ¼-inch-thick medallions
- Salt, as required
- 3 tablespoons sesame oil

For Dressing:

- 2 small red chiles, sliced thinly
- 1/3 cups fresh lime juice
- 1/3 cups fish sauce
- 2 tablespoons brown sugar

For Salad:

- 2½ ounces fried egg noodle
- 1 cup cabbage, sliced thinly
- 1 cup bean sprouts
- 1 cup carrot, peeled and grated
- ½ cup cherry tomatoes, halved
- ½ cup cucumber, sliced thinly
- 1/3 cups scallions, chopped
- 1 cup fresh cilantro leaves, chopped
- 1 cup fresh basil, chopped
- 2 tablespoons peanuts, toasted

Method:

1. Plug in the Power XL Grill Air Fryer Combo.
2. Fill the inner pot with water.
3. Rotate the "Control Knob" to select "Sous Vide" mode.
4. Press "Timer Button" and rotate the "Control Knob" to set the time for 15 minutes.
5. Now press "Temp Button" and rotate the "Control Knob" to set the temperature to 131 degrees F.
6. Close the Power XL Grill Air Fryer Combo with "Glass Lid" and press "Start Button" to preheat.
7. Meanwhile, season the salmon fillets with salt.
8. In a cooking pouch, place the trout pieces.
9. Seal the pouch tightly after squeezing out the excess air.
10. When the unit shows "Add Food", open the lid and place the pouch in inner pot.

11. Close the lid and press "Start Button" to start cooking.
12. When the cooking time is completed, press "Cancel Button" to stop cooking.
13. Open the lid and remove the pouch from inner pot.
14. Carefully open the pouch and transfer the trout pieces onto a plate.
15. With paper towels, pat dry the salmon pieces and then cut into bite-sized pieces.
16. For dressing: in a bowl, add all ingredients and beat until well combined.
17. In a large salad bowl, add all salad ingredients, trout pieces and dressing and toss to coat well.
18. Serve immediately.

Nutritional Information per Serving:

- Calories 421
- Total Fat 24 g
- Saturated Fat 3.6 g
- Cholesterol 63 mg
- Sodium 2000 mg
- Total Carbs 24.7 g
- Fiber 3.3 g
- Sugar 11.3 g
- Protein 28.5 g

Prawn Salad

Preparation Time: 20 minutes
Cooking Time: 15 minutes
Servings: 3

Ingredients:

For Salad:

- 20 prawns, peeled and deveined
- 4 cups romaine lettuce, chopped
- 1 avocado, peeled, pitted and chopped
- 1 cup cherry tomatoes, halved
- 2 cups scallions, chopped

For Dressing:

- 2 tablespoons mayonnaise
- 1 tablespoon ketchup
- 2 teaspoons fresh lemon juice
- 1-2 drops Tabasco sauce

Method:

1. Plug in the Power XL Grill Air Fryer Combo.
2. Fill the inner pot with water.
3. Rotate the "Control Knob" to select "Sous Vide" mode.
4. Press "Timer Button" and rotate the "Control Knob" to set the time for 15 minutes.
5. Now press "Temp Button" and rotate the "Control Knob" to set the temperature to 149 degrees F.
6. Close the Power XL Grill Air Fryer Combo with "Glass Lid" and press "Start Button" to preheat.
7. Meanwhile, season the salmon fillets with the salt.
8. In a cooking pouch, place the prawns.
9. Seal the pouch tightly after squeezing out the excess air.
10. When unit shows "Add Food", open the lid and place the pouch in inner pot.
11. Close the lid and press "Start Button" to start cooking.
12. When the cooking time is completed, press "Cancel Button" to stop cooking.
13. Open the lid and remove the pouch from inner pot.
14. Carefully open the pouch and transfer the prawns into a bowl.
15. In a large bowl, mix together remaining salad ingredients.
16. For dressing: in another bowl, add all ingredients and mix until well combined.
17. In the bowl of dressing, add the prawns and stir to combine.

18. Divide the veggie mixture onto serving plates.
19. Top with prawns and serve.

Nutritional Information per Serving:

- Calories 397
- Total Fat 19.3 g
- Saturated Fat 4.1 g
- Cholesterol 311 mg
- Sodium 506 mg
- Total Carbs 21.1 g
- Fiber 7.4 g
- Sugar 6 g
- Protein 37 g

Seafood Soup

Preparation Time: 20 minutes
Cooking Time: 2½ hours
Servings: 8

Ingredients:

- 6 cups chicken broth
- 3 tablespoons olive oil
- 1 medium onion, chopped
- ½ cup carrot, peeled and chopped
- ½ cup celery stalk, chopped
- 6 cups fresh spinach, chopped
- 1 cup fresh tomatoes, chopped finely
- 1 cup fresh parsley, chopped
- 1 teaspoon garlic powder
- Salt and ground black pepper, as required
- 2 pounds salmon fillets, cubed
- 2 pounds sea mussels, removed beards and scrubbed
- 1 pound large shrimp, peeled and deveined
- 3 tablespoons fresh lime juice
- ¼ cup scallion, chopped

Method:

1. Plug in the Power XL Grill Air Fryer Combo.
2. In the inner pot, add all the ingredients except for seafood, lime juice and scallion and mix well.
3. Rotate the "Control Knob" to select "Slow Cook" mode.
4. Press "Timer Button" and rotate the "Control Knob" to set the time for 2½ hours.
5. Close the Power XL Grill Air Fryer Combo with "Glass Lid" and press "Start Button" to start cooking.
6. After ¾ hours of cooking, open the lid and place salmon over vegetable mixture, followed by mussels and shrimp.
7. When the cooking time is completed, press "Cancel Button" to stop cooking.
8. Open the lid and stir in the lime juice.
9. Serve hot with the topping of scallion.

Nutritional Information per Serving:

- Calories 2391
- Total Fat 16.1 g
- Saturated Fat 12.8 g
- Cholesterol 163 mg
- Sodium 1330 mg
- Total Carbs 10.7 g
- Fiber 1.7 g
- Sugar 2.4 g
- Protein 51.2 g

Salmon & Veggie Stew

Preparation Time: 15 minutes
Cooking Time: 5 hours
Servings: 4

Ingredients:

- 1 pound salmon fillet, cubed
- 1 tablespoon coconut oil
- 1 medium yellow onion, chopped
- 1 garlic clove, minced
- 1 zucchini, sliced
- 1 green bell pepper, seeded and cubed
- ½ cup tomatoes, chopped
- ½ cup fish broth
- ¼ teaspoons dried oregano
- ¼ teaspoons dried basil
- Salt and ground black pepper, as required

Method:

1. Plug in the Power XL Grill Air Fryer Combo.
2. In the inner pot, add all the ingredients and stir to combine.
3. Rotate the "Control Knob" to select "Slow Cook" mode.
4. Press "Timer Button" and rotate the "Control Knob" to set the time for 5 hours.
5. Close the Power XL Grill Air Fryer Combo with "Glass Lid" and press "Start Button" to start cooking.
6. When the cooking time is completed, press "Cancel Button" to stop cooking.
7. Open the lid and serve hot.

Nutritional Information per Serving:

- Calories 218
- Total Fat 10.6 g
- Saturated Fat 4 g
- Cholesterol 50 mg
- Sodium 142 mg
- Total Carbs 7.7 g
- Fiber 1.9 g
- Sugar 4.1 g
- Protein 24.1 g

Lemony Salmon

Preparation Time: 10 minutes
Cooking Time: 8 minutes
Servings: 4

Ingredients:

- 1½ pounds salmon fillets
- ½ teaspoon red chili powder
- Salt and ground black pepper, as required
- 1 lemon, cut into slices

Method:

1. Season the salmon with chili powder, salt, and black pepper evenly.
2. Plug in the Power XL Grill Air Fryer Combo.
3. Rotate the "Control Knob" to select "Air Fry" mode.
4. Press "Timer Button" and rotate the "Control Knob" to set the time for 8 minutes.
5. Now press "Temp Button" and rotate the "Control Knob" to set the temperature to 375 degrees F.
6. Close the Power XL Grill Air Fryer Combo with "Air Frying Lid" and press "Start Button" to preheat.
7. When the unit shows "Add Food", open the lid and arrange the salmon fillets into the greased inner pot.
8. Place the lemon slices over salmon fillets.
9. Close the lid and press "Start Button" to start cooking.
10. When the cooking time is completed, press "Cancel Button" to stop cooking.
11. Open the lid and serve hot.

Nutritional Information per Serving:

- Calories 227
- Total Fat 11.6 g
- Saturated Fat 1.5 g
- Cholesterol 75 mg
- Sodium 117 mg
- Total Carbs 0.5 g
- Fiber 0.2 g
- Sugar 0.1 g
- Protein 33.1 g

Honey Glazed Salmon

Preparation Time: 10 minutes
Cooking Time: 13 minutes
Servings: 2

Ingredients:

- 3 tablespoons low-sodium soy sauce
- 2 tablespoons honey
- 2 teaspoons fresh lemon juice
- 2 teaspoons water
- 2 (4-ounce) salmon fillets

Method:

1. In a small bowl, place all the ingredients except the salmon and mix well.
2. In a small bowl, reserve about half of the mixture.
3. Add the salmon in the remaining mixture and coat well.
4. Refrigerate, covered to marinate for about 2 hours.
5. Plug in the Power XL Grill Air Fryer Combo.
6. Rotate the "Control Knob" to select "Air Fry" mode.
7. Press "Timer Button" and rotate the "Control Knob" to set the time for 13 minutes.
8. Now press "Temp Button" and rotate the "Control Knob" to set the temperature to 355 degrees F.
9. Close the Power XL Grill Air Fryer Combo with "Air Frying Lid" and press "Start Button" to preheat.
10. When the unit shows "Add Food", open the lid and arrange the salmon fillets into the greased inner pot.
11. Close the lid and press "Start Button" to start cooking.
12. When the cooking time is completed, press "Cancel Button" to stop cooking.
13. Open the lid and serve hot.

Nutritional Information per Serving:

- Calories 223
- Total Fat 7 g
- Saturated Fat 1 g
- Cholesterol 45 mg
- Sodium 1300 mg
- Total Carbs 16.9 g
- Fiber 0.1 g
- Sugar 18.9 g
- Protein 23.6 g

Buttered Salmon

Preparation Time: 10 minutes
Cooking Time: 30 minutes
Servings: 4

Ingredients:

- 1 pound salmon fillets
- 1 tablespoon ginger paste
- 1 tablespoon garlic paste
- Salt and ground black pepper, as required
- 3 jalapeño peppers, chopped
- ¾ cup butter, chopped

Method:

1. Coat the salmon fillets with ginger-garlic paste and then season with salt and black pepper.
2. Plug in the Power XL Grill Air Fryer Combo.
3. Rotate the "Control Knob" to select "Air Fry" mode.
4. Press "Timer Button" and rotate the "Control Knob" to set the time for 30 minutes.
5. Now press "Temp Button" and rotate the "Control Knob" to set the temperature to 380 degrees F.
6. Close the Power XL Grill Air Fryer Combo with "Air Frying Lid" and press "Start Button" to preheat.
7. When the unit shows "Add Food", open the lid and arrange the salmon fillets into the greased inner pot.
8. Top each fillet with jalapeño pepper pieces, followed by the butter.
9. Close the lid and press "Start Button" to start cooking.
10. When the cooking time is completed, press "Cancel Button" to stop cooking.
11. Open the lid and serve hot.

Nutritional Information per Serving:

- Calories 467
- Total Fat 41.8 g
- Saturated Fat 22.8 g
- Cholesterol 145 mg
- Sodium 610 mg
- Total Carbs 2.5 g
- Fiber 0.6 g
- Sugar 0.5 g
- Protein 22.8 g

Cajun Herring

Preparation Time: 5 minutes
Cooking Time: 8 minutes
Servings: 2

Ingredients:

- 2 (6-ounce) salmon steaks
- 2 tablespoons Cajun seasoning

Method:

1. Rub the salmon steaks with the Cajun seasoning evenly and set aside for about 10 minutes.
2. Plug in the Power XL Grill Air Fryer Combo.
3. Rotate the "Control Knob" to select "Air Fry" mode.
4. Press "Timer Button" and rotate the "Control Knob" to set the time for 8 minutes.
5. Now press "Temp Button" and rotate the "Control Knob" to set the temperature to 390 degrees F.
6. Close the Power XL Grill Air Fryer Combo with "Air Frying Lid" and press "Start Button" to preheat.
7. When the unit shows "Add Food", open the lid and arrange the salmon steaks into the greased inner pot.
8. Close the lid and press "Start Button" to start cooking.
9. After 4 minutes of cooking, flip the salmon steaks.
10. When the cooking time is completed, press "Cancel Button" to stop cooking.
11. Open the lid and serve hot.

Nutritional Information per Serving:

- Calories 225
- Total Fat 11 g
- Saturated Fat 1.5 g
- Cholesterol 75 mg
- Sodium 225 mg
- Total Carbs 0 g
- Fiber 0 g
- Sugar 0 g
- Protein 33.1 g

Halibut in Herb Sauce

Preparation Time: 10 minutes
Cooking Time: 2 hours
Servings: 6

Ingredients:

- 2 cups water
- 1 cup chicken broth
- 2 tablespoons fresh lime juice
- ¼ cup fresh parsley, chopped
- ½ teaspoon lime zest, grated
- 6 (4-ounce) halibut fillets
- 1 teaspoon cayenne pepper
- Salt and ground black pepper, as required

Method:

1. Plug in the Power XL Grill Air Fryer Combo.
2. In the inner pot, mix together the water, broth, lime juice, parsley and lime zest.
3. Arrange the halibut fillets on top, skin side down and sprinkle with cayenne pepper, salt black pepper.
4. Rotate the "Control Knob" to select "Slow Cook" mode.
5. Press "Timer Button" and rotate the "Control Knob" to set the time for 2 hours.
6. Close the Power XL Grill Air Fryer Combo with "Glass Lid" and press "Start Button" to start cooking.
7. When the cooking time is completed, press "Cancel Button" to stop cooking.
8. Open the lid and serve hot.

Nutritional Information per Serving:

- Calories 135
- Total Fat 3 g
- Saturated Fat 0.4 g
- Cholesterol 36 mg
- Sodium 218 mg
- Total Carbs 0.6 g
- Fiber 0.2 g
- Sugar 0.2 g
- Protein 24.8 g

Breaded Hake

Preparation Time: 10 minutes
Cooking Time: 10 minutes
Servings: 4

Ingredients:

- 1/3 cups all-purpose flour
- Freshly ground black pepper, as required
- 1 large egg
- 2 tablespoons water
- 2/3 cups cornflakes, crushed
- 1 tablespoon Parmesan cheese, grated
- 1/8 teaspoons cayenne pepper
- 1 pound hake fillets
- Salt, as required

Method:

1. In a shallow dish, place the flour and black pepper and mix well.
2. In a second shallow dish, add the egg and water and beat well.
3. In a third shallow dish, add the cornflakes, cheese and cayenne pepper and mix until well combined.
4. Season the hake fillets with salt evenly.
5. Coat each hake fillet with flour mixture, then dip into egg mixture and finally coat with the cornflake mixture.
6. Plug in the Power XL Grill Air Fryer Combo.
7. Rotate the "Control Knob" to select "Air Fry" mode.
8. Press "Timer Button" and rotate the "Control Knob" to set the time for 10 minutes.
9. Now press "Temp Button" and rotate the "Control Knob" to set the temperature to 360 degrees F.
10. Close the Power XL Grill Air Fryer Combo with "Air Frying Lid" and press "Start Button" to preheat.
11. When the unit shows "Add Food", open the lid and arrange the hake fillets into the greased inner pot.
12. Close the lid and press "Start Button" to start cooking.
13. When the cooking time is completed, press "Cancel Button" to stop cooking.
14. Open the lid and serve hot.

Nutritional Information per Serving:

- Calories 188
- Total Fat 4.6 g
- Saturated Fat 1.8 g
- Cholesterol 50 mg
- Sodium 279 mg
- Total Carbs 14.2 g
- Fiber 1.2 g
- Sugar 1.1 g
- Protein 22.6 g

Sweet & Sour Cod

Preparation Time: 15 minutes
Cooking Time: 15 minutes
Servings: 4

Ingredients:

- 1 garlic clove, minced
- ¼ teaspoons fresh ginger, grated finely
- ½ cup low-sodium soy sauce
- ¼ cup fresh lime juice
- ½ cup chicken broth
- ¼ cup sugar
- ¼ teaspoons red pepper flakes, crushed
- 1 pound cod fillets

Method:

1. Plug in the Power XL Grill Air Fryer Combo and place all ingredients except for cod in the inner pot.
2. Rotate the "Control Knob" to select "Sauté" mode and press "Start Button" to start cooking.
3. Cook for about 3-4 minutes, stirring frequently with a wooden spoon.
4. Press "Cancel Button" to stop cooking and transfer the garlic mixture into a bowl. Set aside to cool.
5. In a bowl, reserve half of the garlic mixture.
6. In a resealable bag, add the remaining garlic mixture and cod fillets.
7. Seal the bag and shake to coat well.
8. Refrigerate for about 30 minutes.
9. Plug in the Power XL Grill Air Fryer Combo.
10. Rotate the "Control Knob" to select "Air Fry" mode.
11. Press "Timer Button" and rotate the "Control Knob" to set the time for 11 minutes.
12. Now press "Temp Button" and rotate the "Control Knob" to set the temperature to 390 degrees F.
13. Close the Power XL Grill Air Fryer Combo with "Air Frying Lid" and press "Start Button" to preheat.
14. When the unit shows "Add Food", open the lid and arrange the cod fillets into the greased inner pot.
15. Close the lid and press "Start Button" to start cooking.
16. When the cooking time is completed, press "Cancel Button" to stop cooking.
17. Open the lid and transfer the cod fillets onto a serving platter.

18. Immediately coat the cod fillets with the reserved garlic mixture.
19. Serve immediately.

Nutritional Information per Serving:

- Calories 156
- Total Fat 1.6 g
- Saturated Fat 0.1 g
- Cholesterol 56 mg
- Sodium 1334 mg
- Total Carbs 15.2 g
- Fiber 0.1 g
- Sugar 14.6 g
- Protein 22.9 g

Vanilla & Paprika Shrimp

Preparation Time: 10 minutes
Cooking Time: 30 minutes
Servings: 3

Ingredients:

- 1 vanilla bean
- 1 pound shrimp, peeled and deveined
- ¼ teaspoons paprika
- Salt and ground black pepper, as required

Method:

1. Plug in the Power XL Grill Air Fryer Combo.
2. Fill the inner pot with water.
3. Rotate the "Control Knob" to select "Sous Vide" mode.
4. Press "Timer Button" and rotate the "Control Knob" to set the time for 30 minutes.
5. Now press "Temp Button" and rotate the "Control Knob" to set the temperature to 136 degrees F.
6. Close the Power XL Grill Air Fryer Combo with "Glass Lid" and press "Start Button" to preheat.
7. Meanwhile, split the vanilla bean in half and scrape out the seeds.
8. In a bowl, add shrimp, vanilla seeds, paprika, salt and pepper and toss to coat.
9. In a cooking pouch, place the shrimp mixture.
10. Seal the pouch tightly after squeezing out the excess air.
11. When the unit shows "Add Food", open the lid and place the pouch in inner pot.
12. Close the lid and press "Start Button" to start cooking.
13. When the cooking time is completed, press "Cancel Button" to stop cooking.
14. Open the lid and remove the pouch from inner pot.
15. Carefully open the pouch and transfer the shrimp with cooking liquid into a serving bowl.
16. Serve hot.

Nutritional Information per Serving:

- Calories 180
- Total Fat 2.6 g
- Saturated Fat 0.8 g
- Cholesterol 318 mg
- Sodium 4194 mg
- Total Carbs 2.4 g
- Fiber 0.1 g
- Sugar 0 g

- Protein 34.5 g

Garlicky Butter Shrimp

Preparation Time: 15 minutes
Cooking Time: 50 minutes
Servings: 6

Ingredients:

- 8 garlic cloves, chopped
- ¼ cup fresh cilantro, chopped
- 1/3 cup unsalted butter
- ½ teaspoon lemon pepper
- ¼ teaspoon cayenne pepper
- Salt and ground black pepper, as required
- 2 pounds extra-large shrimp, peeled and deveined

Method:

1. Plug in the Power XL Grill Air Fryer Combo.
2. In the inner pot, add all ingredients except for shrimp and stir to combine.
3. Rotate the "Control Knob" to select "Slow Cook" mode.
4. Press "Timer Button" and rotate the "Control Knob" to set the time for 50 minutes.
5. Close the Power XL Grill Air Fryer Combo with "Glass Lid" and press "Start Button" to start cooking.
6. After 30 minutes of cooking, open the lid and stir in the shrimp.
7. When the cooking time is completed, press "Cancel Button" to stop cooking.
8. Open the lid and serve hot.

Nutritional Information per Serving:

- Calories 277
- Total Fat 12.8 g
- Saturated Fat 7.3 g
- Cholesterol 345 mg
- Sodium 470 mg
- Total Carbs 3.8 g
- Fiber 0.2 g
- Sugar 0.1 g
- Protein 34.8 g

Shrimp with Bell Peppers

Preparation Time: 15 minutes
Cooking Time: 3 hours
Servings: 6

Ingredients:

- 1 cup red bell pepper, seeded and sliced
- 1 cup green bell pepper, seeded and sliced
- 2 cups tomatoes, chopped finely
- 1 garlic clove, minced
- 1 cup tomato sauce
- ½ teaspoon dried thyme, crushed
- ½ teaspoon dried basil, crushed
- ¼ teaspoon cayenne pepper
- 1 teaspoon lemon pepper
- ¼ teaspoon red pepper flakes, crushed
- Salt and ground black pepper, as required
- 1½ pounds large shrimp, peeled and deveined

Method:

1. Plug in the Power XL Grill Air Fryer Combo.
2. In the inner pot, add all ingredients except for shrimp and stir to combine.
3. Rotate the "Control Knob" to select "Slow Cook" mode.
4. Press "Timer Button" and rotate the "Control Knob" to set the time for 3 hours.
5. Close the Power XL Grill Air Fryer Combo with "Glass Lid" and press "Start Button" to start cooking.
6. After 2½ hours of cooking, open the lid and stir in the shrimp.
7. When the cooking time is completed, press "Cancel Button" to stop cooking.
8. Open the lid and serve hot.

Nutritional Information per Serving:

- Calories 170
- Total Fat 2.2 g
- Saturated Fat 0.6 g
- Cholesterol 239 mg
- Sodium 522 mg
- Total Carbs 9.8 g
- Fiber 2 g
- Sugar 27.4 g
- Protein: 30.1 g

Buttered Scallops

Preparation Time: 10 minutes
Cooking Time: 4 minutes
Servings: 2

Ingredients:

- ¾ pound sea scallops, cleaned and patted very dry
- 1 tablespoon butter, melted
- ½ tablespoon fresh thyme, minced
- Salt and ground black pepper, as required

Method:

1. In a large bowl, place the scallops, butter, thyme, salt, and black pepper and toss to coat well.
2. Plug in the Power XL Grill Air Fryer Combo.
3. Rotate the "Control Knob" to select "Air Fry" mode.
4. Press "Timer Button" and rotate the "Control Knob" to set the time for 4 minutes.
5. Now press "Temp Button" and rotate the "Control Knob" to set the temperature to 390 degrees F.
6. Close the Power XL Grill Air Fryer Combo with "Air Frying Lid" and press "Start Button" to preheat.
7. When the unit shows "Add Food", open the lid and arrange the scallops into the greased inner pot.
8. Close the lid and press "Start Button" to start cooking.
9. When the cooking time is completed, press "Cancel Button" to stop cooking.
10. Open the lid and serve hot.

Nutritional Information per Serving:

- Calories 202
- Total Fat 7.1 g
- Saturated Fat 3.8 g
- Cholesterol 71 mg
- Sodium 393 mg
- Total Carbs 4.4 g
- Fiber 0.3 g
- Sugar 0 g
- Protein 28.7 g

Chapter 8: Vegetarian Recipes

Beet & Feta Salad

Preparation Time: 15 minutes
Cooking Time: 4 hours
Servings: 2

Ingredients:

For Salad:

- 4 medium red beets, trimmed
- 1 tablespoon olive oil
- 3 cups fresh baby spinach
- ¼ teaspoon fresh lemon zest, grated finely
- 1 tablespoon feta cheese, crumbled
- 2 tablespoons walnuts, chopped

For Dressing:

- 2 garlic cloves, minced
- 1 tablespoon fresh cilantro, minced
- 1 tablespoon extra-virgin olive oil
- 1 tablespoon fresh lemon juice
- Salt and ground black pepper, as required

Method:

1. Place each beet over 1 piece of foil.
2. Drizzle each beet with oil.
3. Wrap each piece of foil around beet to seal it.
4. Plug in the Power XL Grill Air Fryer Combo.
5. In the inner pot, place the foil packets.
6. Rotate the "Control Knob" to select "Slow Cook" mode.
7. Press "Timer Button" and rotate the "Control Knob" to set the time for 4 hours.
8. Close the Power XL Grill Air Fryer Combo with "Glass Lid" and press "Start Button" to start cooking.
9. When the cooking time is completed, press "Cancel Button" to stop cooking.
10. Open the lid and transfer the beets into a salad bowl.
11. Let them cool slightly.
12. Peel the bets and cut into desired sized pieces.
13. In the bowl, add the remaining salad ingredients and mix.
14. For dressing: in another bowl, add all ingredients and beat until well combined.
15. Pour dressing over beets and gently toss to coat well.
16. Serve immediately.

Nutritional Information per Serving:

- Calories 286
- Total Fat 20.2 g
- Saturated Fat 3.1 g
- Cholesterol 4 mg
- Sodium 322 mg
- Total Carbs 23.7 g
- Fiber 5.6 g
- Sugar 16.6 g
- Protein 7.5 g

Potato Salad

Preparation Time: 15 minutes
Cooking Time: 45 minutes
Servings: 8

Ingredients:

- 2 pounds red potatoes, cubed
- 1 tablespoon olive oil
- 1 small onion, chopped
- ¼ cup white vinegar
- 2 tablespoons granulated sugar
- ½ teaspoon dry mustard
- Salt and ground black pepper, as required
- ¼ cup fresh parsley, chopped

Method:

1. Plug in the Power XL Grill Air Fryer Combo.
2. Fill the inner pot with water.
3. Rotate the "Control Knob" to select "Sous Vide" mode.
4. Press "Timer Button" and rotate the "Control Knob" to set the time for 45 minutes.
5. Now press "Temp Button" and rotate the "Control Knob" to set the temperature to 182 degrees F.
6. Close the Power XL Grill Air Fryer Combo with "Glass Lid" and press "Start Button" to preheat.
7. Meanwhile, in a cooking pouch, place the potatoes.
8. Seal the pouch tightly after squeezing out the excess air.
9. When the unit shows "Add Food", open the lid and place the pouch in inner pot.
10. Close the lid and press "Start Button" to start cooking.
11. Meanwhile, in a skillet, heat the oil over medium heat and sauté the onion for about 4-5 minutes.
12. Stir in the vinegar and cook for about 1-2 minutes, scraping the brown bits.
13. Add sugar, mustard, salt and black pepper and cook for about 2-3 minutes or until the sugar dissolves, stirring continuously.
14. Remove the skillet of onion mixture from the heat and set aside to cool slightly.
15. When the cooking time is completed, press "Cancel Button" to stop cooking.
16. Open the lid and remove the pouch from inner pot.
17. Carefully open the pouch and transfer into a serving bowl.
18. Place warm dressing and toss to coat.
19. Garnish with parsley and serve.

Nutritional Information per Serving:

- Calories 112
- Total Fat 2 g
- Saturated Fat 0.3 g
- Cholesterol 0 mg
- Sodium 28 mg

- Total Carbs 22.1 g
- Fiber 2.2 g
- Sugar 4.6 g
- Protein 2.4 g

Tomato Soup

Preparation Time: 10 minutes
Cooking Time: 15 minutes
Servings: 4

Ingredients:

- 4 cups fresh tomatoes, cored and halved
- ½ onion, chopped
- 1/3 cup fresh basil, divided
- 2 garlic cloves, minced
- Salt and ground black pepper, as required
- 5 tablespoons extra-virgin olive oil
- 5 tablespoons crème fraiche

Method:

1. Plug in the Power XL Grill Air Fryer Combo.
2. Fill the inner pot with water.
3. Rotate the "Control Knob" to select "Sous Vide" mode.
4. Press "Timer Button" and rotate the "Control Knob" to set the time for 15 minutes.
5. Now press "Temp Button" and rotate the "Control Knob" to set the temperature to 176 degrees F.
6. Close the Power XL Grill Air Fryer Combo with "Glass Lid" and press "Start Button" to preheat.
7. Meanwhile, in a cooking pouch, place the tomatoes, onion, ¼ cup of basil and garlic.
8. Seal the pouch tightly after squeezing out the excess air.
9. When the unit shows "Add Food", open the lid and place the pouch in inner pot.
10. Close the lid and press "Start Button" to start cooking.
11. When the cooking time is completed, press "Cancel Button" to stop cooking.
12. Open the lid and remove the pouch from inner pot.
13. Carefully open the pouch and transfer the tomato mixture into a blender.
14. Add the olive oil, crème fraiche, salt and pepper and pulse until smooth.
15. Serve immediately with the garnishing of remaining basil.

Nutritional Information per Serving:

- Calories 200
- Total Fat 16.7 g
- Saturated Fat 3.1 g
- Cholesterol 3 mg
- Sodium 53 mg
- Total Carbs 9.3 g
- Fiber 2.5 g
- Sugar 5.6 g

- Protein 2 g

Broccoli Soup

Preparation Time: 15 minutes
Cooking Time: 6 hours 10 minutes
Servings: 6

Ingredients:

- 2 tablespoons unsalted butter
- 1 onion, chopped
- 2 garlic cloves, minced
- 1 tablespoon fresh rosemary, chopped
- 4 cups small broccoli florets
- 5 cups vegetable broth
- Salt and ground black pepper, as required
- 1 cup coconut cream

Method:

1. Plug in the Power XL Grill Air Fryer Combo and add the butter in the inner pot.
2. Rotate the "Control Knob" to select "Sauté" mode and press "Start Button" to start cooking.
3. Add onion and cook for about 3-4 minutes.
4. Add garlic and rosemary and sauté for 1 minute.
5. Press "Cancel Button" to stop cooking and stir in the remaining ingredients except for coconut cream.
6. Rotate the "Control Knob" to select "Slow Cook" mode.
7. Press "Timer Button" and rotate the "Control Knob" to set the time for 6 hours.
8. Close the Power XL Grill Air Fryer Combo with "Glass Lid" and press "Start Button" to start cooking.
9. When the cooking time is completed, press "Cancel Button" to stop cooking.
10. Open the lid and stir in the coconut cream.
11. With an immersion blender, blend the soup until smooth.
12. Serve immediately.

Nutritional Information per Serving:

- Calories 375
- Total Fat 32.1 g
- Saturated Fat 24.8 g
- Cholesterol 10 mg
- Sodium 712 mg
- Total Carbs 16 g
- Fiber 2.6 g
- Sugar 2.4 g
- Protein 9 g

Cauliflower Soup

Preparation Time: 10 minutes
Cooking Time: 4 hours
Servings: 4

Ingredients:

- 3 leeks, cut into 1-inch pieces
- 1 large cauliflower head, chopped
- 3 garlic cloves, chopped finely
- 4 cups vegetable broth
- 2 tablespoon fresh basil, chopped
- Salt and ground black pepper, as required

Method:

1. Plug in the Power XL Grill Air Fryer Combo.
2. In the inner pot, add all the ingredients and stir to combine.
3. Rotate the "Control Knob" to select "Slow Cook" mode.
4. Press "Timer Button" and rotate the "Control Knob" to set the time for 4 hours.
5. Close the Power XL Grill Air Fryer Combo with "Glass Lid" and press "Start Button" to start cooking.
6. When the cooking time is completed, press "Cancel Button" to stop cooking.
7. Open the lid and serve hot

Nutritional Information per Serving:

- Calories 99
- Total Fat 1.6 g
- Saturated Fat 0.4 g
- Cholesterol 0 mg
- Sodium 834 mg
- Total Carbs 14.7 g
- Fiber 2.9 g
- Sugar 4.9 g
- Protein 7.3 g

Squash with Fruit

Preparation Time: 15 minutes
Cooking Time: 4 hours
Servings: 8

Ingredients:

- 3 apples, peeled, cored and chopped
- 1 (3 pounds) butternut squash, peeled, seeded and cubed
- ½ cup dried cranberries
- ½ of white onion, chopped
- ¼ teaspoon dried rosemary
- ½ teaspoon garlic powder
- 1 tablespoon ground cinnamon
- Salt and ground black pepper, as required

Method:

1. Plug in the Power XL Grill Air Fryer Combo.
2. In the inner pot, add all the ingredients and mix well.
3. Rotate the "Control Knob" to select "Slow Cook" mode.
4. Press "Timer Button" and rotate the "Control Knob" to set the time for 4 hours.
5. Close the Power XL Grill Air Fryer Combo with "Glass Lid" and press "Start Button" to start cooking.
6. When the cooking time is completed, press "Cancel Button" to stop cooking.
7. Open the lid and serve warm.

Nutritional Information per Serving:

- Calories 129
- Total Fat 0.4 g
- Saturated Fat 0 g
- Cholesterol 0 mg
- Sodium 27 mg
- Total Carbs 33.6 g
- Fiber 6.3 g
- Sugar 12 g
- Protein 2.1 g

Cheesy Spinach

Preparation Time: 10 minutes
Cooking Time: 1 hour
Servings: 5

Ingredients:

- 3 ounces cream cheese, softened
- 16 ounces fresh baby spinach
- 1 cup cheddar cheese, shredded
- Salt and ground black pepper, as required

Method:

1. Plug in the Power XL Grill Air Fryer Combo.
2. In the inner pot, place the cream cheese and top with spinach, followed by cheddar cheese.
3. Rotate the "Control Knob" to select "Slow Cook" mode.
4. Press "Timer Button" and rotate the "Control Knob" to set the time for 1 hour.
5. Close the Power XL Grill Air Fryer Combo with "Glass Lid" and press "Start Button" to start cooking.
6. When the cooking time is completed, press "Cancel Button" to stop cooking.
7. Open the lid and stir in salt and black pepper.
8. Serve hot.

Nutritional Information per Serving:

- Calories 171
- Total Fat 13.8 g
- Saturated Fat 8.5 g
- Cholesterol 45 mg
- Sodium 294 mg
- Total Carbs 4 g
- Fiber 2 g
- Sugar 0.5 g
- Protein 9.5 g

Garlicky Brussels Sprout

Preparation Time: 10 minutes
Cooking Time: 1 hour 6 minutes
Servings: 3

Ingredients:

- 1 tablespoon olive oil
- 2 garlic cloves, smashed and minced
- Salt and ground black pepper, as required
- 1 pound Brussels sprouts, trimmed

Method:

1. Plug in the Power XL Grill Air Fryer Combo.
2. Fill the inner pot with water.
3. Rotate the "Control Knob" to select "Sous Vide" mode.
4. Press "Timer Button" and rotate the "Control Knob" to set the time for 1 hour.
5. Now press "Temp Button" and rotate the "Control Knob" to set the temperature to 180 degrees F.
6. Close the Power XL Grill Air Fryer Combo with "Glass Lid" and press "Start Button" to preheat.
7. Meanwhile, in a bowl, add all ingredients except for Brussels sprouts and mix until well combined.
8. In a cooking pouch, place Brussels sprouts and oil mixture.
9. Seal the pouch tightly after squeezing out the excess air.
10. When the unit shows "Add Food", open the lid and place the pouch in inner pot.
11. Close the lid and press "Start Button" to start cooking.
12. When the cooking time is completed, press "Cancel Button" to stop cooking.
13. Open the lid and remove the pouch from inner pot.
14. Carefully open the pouch and serve immediately.

Nutritional Information per Serving:

- Calories 108
- Total Fat 5.2 g
- Saturated Fat 0.8 g
- Cholesterol 0 mg
- Sodium 89 mg
- Total Carbs 14.4 g
- Fiber 6.7 g
- Sugar 3.3 g
- Protein 5.3 g

Mushrooms in Sauce

Preparation Time: 10 minutes
Cooking Time: 10 minutes
Servings: 3

Ingredients:

- 1 pound fresh mixed mushrooms (lobster, porcini and shitake), cut into bite-sized pieces
- 1 tablespoon mirin
- 1 tablespoon soy sauce
- 1 tablespoon oyster sauce
- 2 teaspoons fresh ginger, chopped finely
- Ground black pepper, as required
- 2 tablespoons fresh cilantro, chopped

Method:

1. Plug in the Power XL Grill Air Fryer Combo.
2. Fill the inner pot with water.
3. Rotate the "Control Knob" to select "Sous Vide" mode.
4. Press "Timer Button" and rotate the "Control Knob" to set the time for 10 minutes.
5. Now press "Temp Button" and rotate the "Control Knob" to set the temperature to 185 degrees F.
6. Close the Power XL Grill Air Fryer Combo with "Glass Lid" and press "Start Button" to preheat.
7. Meanwhile, in a cooking pouch, place all ingredients except for the cilantro.
8. Seal the pouch tightly after squeezing out the excess air.
9. When the unit shows "Add Food", open the lid and place the pouch in inner pot.
10. Close the lid and press "Start Button" to start cooking.
11. When the cooking time is completed, press "Cancel Button" to stop cooking.
12. Open the lid and remove the pouch from inner pot.
13. Carefully open the pouch and transfer the mushrooms with cooking liquid into a serving bowl.
14. Top with cilantro and serve.

Nutritional Information per Serving:

- Calories 49
- Total Fat 0.5 g
- Saturated Fat 0 g
- Cholesterol 0 mg
- Sodium 390 mg
- Total Carbs 8.8 g
- Fiber 1.7 g
- Sugar 4.1 g

- Protein 5.2 g

Herbed Bell Peppers

Preparation Time: 10 minutes
Cooking Time: 8 minutes
Servings: 5

Ingredients:

- 1½ pounds bell peppers, seeded and cubed
- ½ teaspoon dried thyme, crushed
- ½ teaspoon dried savory, crushed
- Salt and ground black pepper, as required
- 2 teaspoons butter, melted

Method:

1. In a bowl, add the bell peppers, herbs, salt and black pepper and toss to coat well.
2. Plug in the Power XL Grill Air Fryer Combo.
3. Rotate the "Control Knob" to select "Air Fry" mode.
4. Press "Timer Button" and rotate the "Control Knob" to set the time for 8 minutes.
5. Now press "Temp Button" and rotate the "Control Knob" to set the temperature to 360 degrees F.
6. Close the Power XL Grill Air Fryer Combo with "Air Frying Lid" and press "Start Button" to preheat.
7. When the unit shows "Add Food", open the lid and arrange the bell peppers into the greased inner pot.
8. Close the lid and press "Start Button" to start cooking.
9. When the cooking time is completed, press "Cancel Button" to stop cooking.
10. Open the lid and transfer the bell peppers into a bowl.
11. Drizzle with butter and serve immediately.

Nutritional Information per Serving:

- Calories 26
- Total Fat 1.6 g
- Saturated Fat 1 g
- Cholesterol 4 mg
- Sodium 44 mg
- Total Carbs 2.9 g
- Fiber 0.6 g
- Sugar 1.8 g
- Protein 0.4 g

Curried Cauliflower

Preparation Time: 15 minutes
Cooking Time: 3 hours
Servings: 4

Ingredients:

For Curry Sauce:

- 2 cups vegetable broth
- 2 cups unsweetened coconut milk
- 2 tablespoons yellow curry powder
- 1 teaspoon ground cumin
- ½ teaspoon cayenne pepper

For Cauliflower:

- 1 large cauliflower head, trimmed leaves and stems
- 2 small red potatoes, quartered
- 1 bell pepper, seeded and sliced thinly
- ½ of onion, chopped
- 2 garlic cloves, sliced
- 2 tablespoons cashews, toasted

Method:

1. For curry sauce: in a bowl, add all ingredients and beat until well combined.
2. Plug in the Power XL Grill Air Fryer Combo.
3. In the inner pot, place whole cauliflower, potatoes, bell peppers, onion and garlic.
4. Pour curry sauce eon top and stir well.
5. Rotate the "Control Knob" to select "Slow Cook" mode.
6. Press "Timer Button" and rotate the "Control Knob" to set the time for 3 hours.
7. Close the Power XL Grill Air Fryer Combo with "Glass Lid" and press "Start Button" to start cooking.
8. In the last 10-15 minutes of cooking, stir in coconut milk.
9. When the cooking time is completed, press "Cancel Button" to stop cooking.
10. Open the lid and transfer the cauliflower head onto a plate.
11. Cut the cauliflower head into wedges.
12. Divide cauliflower onto plates and top with the curry sauce and cashews.
13. Serve immediately.

Nutritional Information per Serving:

- Calories 340
- Total Fat 23.1 g
- Saturated Fat 18.6 g
- Cholesterol 0 mg
- Sodium 460 mg
- Total Carbs 29.3 g
- Fiber 4.1 g
- Sugar 7.1 g
- Protein 7.7 g

Broccoli in Cheesy Sauce

Preparation Time: 10 minutes
Cooking Time: 7 hours
Servings: 10

Ingredients:

- 8 cups broccoli florets
- 1 large onion, chopped
- ½ tablespoon fresh rosemary, minced
- ½ tablespoon fresh parsley, chopped
- 1½ cups Swiss cheese, torn
- 1¾ cups tomato sauce
- 1 tablespoon fresh lemon juice
- Salt and ground black pepper, as required

Method:

1. Plug in the Power XL Grill Air Fryer Combo.
2. In the inner pot, add all the ingredients and stir to combine.
3. Rotate the "Control Knob" to select "Slow Cook" mode.
4. Press "Timer Button" and rotate the "Control Knob" to set the time for 7 hours.
5. Close the Power XL Grill Air Fryer Combo with "Glass Lid" and press "Start Button" to start cooking.
6. When the cooking time is completed, press "Cancel Button" to stop cooking.
7. Open the lid and serve hot.

Nutritional Information per Serving:

- Calories 104
- Total Fat 4.9 g
- Saturated Fat 2.9 g
- Cholesterol 15 mg
- Sodium 296 mg
- Total Carbs 9.6 g
- Fiber 2.9 g
- Sugar 3.9 g
- Protein 7.2 g

Chapter 9: Snack Recipes

Deviled Eggs

Preparation Time: 15 minutes
Cooking Time: 20 minutes
Servings: 8

Ingredients:

- 8 large eggs
- 3 tablespoons mayonnaise
- 1 tablespoon of Dijon mustard
- Pinch of sugar
- Salt and ground black pepper, as required
- Cayenne pepper, as required

Method:

1. Plug in the Power XL Grill Air Fryer Combo.
2. Fill the inner pot with water.
3. Rotate the "Control Knob" to select "Sous Vide" mode.
4. Press "Timer Button" and rotate the "Control Knob" to set the time for 20 minutes.
5. Now press "Temp Button" and rotate the "Control Knob" to set the temperature to 170 degrees F.
6. Close the Power XL Grill Air Fryer Combo with "Glass Lid" and press "Start Button" to preheat.
7. Meanwhile, in a cooking pouch, place the eggs.
8. Seal the pouch tightly after squeezing out the excess air.
9. When the unit shows "Add Food", open the lid and place the pouch in inner pot.
10. Close the lid and press "Start Button" to start cooking.
11. When the cooking time is completed, press "Cancel Button" to stop cooking.
12. Open the lid and remove the pouch from inner pot.
13. Carefully open the pouch and transfer the eggs into an ice bath for about 20 minutes.
14. Peel the eggs and cut in half lengthwise.
15. Remove the yolks and transfer into a bowl.
16. Add the mayonnaise, Dijon mustard, sugar, salt and pepper and mash well.
17. Fill the egg halves with yolk mixture.
18. Sprinkle with cayenne pepper and serve.

Nutritional Information per Serving:

- Calories 95
- Total Fat 6.9 g
- Saturated Fat 1.8 g
- Cholesterol 187 mg
- Sodium 151 mg
- Total Carbs 1.9 g
- Fiber 0.1 g
- Sugar 0.8 g
- Protein 6.4 g

Roasted Cashews

Preparation Time: 5 minutes
Cooking Time: 5 minutes
Servings: 8

Ingredients:

- 2 cups raw cashew nuts
- 1 tablespoon olive oil
- Salt and ground black pepper, as required

Method:

1. In a bowl, mix together all the ingredients.
2. Plug in the Power XL Grill Air Fryer Combo.
3. Rotate the "Control Knob" to select "Air Fry" mode.
4. Press "Timer Button" and rotate the "Control Knob" to set the time for 5 minutes.
5. Now press "Temp Button" and rotate the "Control Knob" to set the temperature to 355 degrees F.
6. Close the Power XL Grill Air Fryer Combo with "Air Frying Lid" and press "Start Button" to preheat.
7. When the unit shows "Add Food", open the lid and arrange the cashews into the greased inner pot.
8. Close the lid and press "Start Button" to start cooking.
9. Shake the cashews once halfway through.
10. When the cooking time is completed, press "Cancel Button" to stop cooking.
11. Open the lid and transfer the cashews into a bowl.
12. Serve warm.

Nutritional Information per Serving:

- Calories 212
- Total Fat 17.6 g
- Saturated Fat 3.4 g
- Cholesterol 0 mg
- Sodium 25 mg
- Total Carbs 11.2 g
- Fiber 1 g
- Sugar 1.7 g
- Protein 5.2 g

Candied Pecans

Preparation Time: 10 minutes
Cooking Time: 3½ hours
Servings: 8

Ingredients:

- 2 cups pecan halves
- ½ cup sugar
- ½ cup brown sugar
- 1 tablespoon ground cinnamon
- 1/8 teaspoon salt
- 2 egg whites
- 1¼ teaspoons vanilla extract

Method:

1. In a large bowl, mix together sugar, brown sugar, cinnamon, and salt.
2. In another bowl, add egg whites and vanilla extract and beat until foamy.
3. Dip the pecans to the egg mixture and then coat with cinnamon sugar mixture.
4. Plug in the Power XL Grill Air Fryer Combo.
5. In the inner pot, place the pecans.
6. Rotate the "Control Knob" to select "Slow Cook" mode.
7. Press "Timer Button" and rotate the "Control Knob" to set the time for 3½ hours.
8. Close the Power XL Grill Air Fryer Combo with "Glass Lid" and press "Start Button" to start cooking.
9. When the cooking time is completed, press "Cancel Button" to stop cooking.
10. Open the lid and transfer the pecans into a bowl.
11. Serve warm.

Nutritional Information per Serving:

- Calories 307
- Total Fat 22.3 g
- Saturated Fat 2.2 g
- Cholesterol 0 mg
- Sodium 47 mg
- Total Carbs 25.7 g
- Fiber 3.8 g
- Sugar 22.6 g
- Protein 4.3 g

Glazed Corn

Preparation Time: 10 minutes
Cooking Time: 22 minutes
Servings: 3

Ingredients:

- 3 ears of summer corn
- 3 garlic cloves
- 1 scallion, chopped roughly
- 2 tablespoons butter
- 3 tablespoons dark soy sauce
- 2 tablespoons chili sauce
- 1 tablespoon sugar

Method:

1. Plug in the Power XL Grill Air Fryer Combo.
2. Fill the inner pot with water.
3. Rotate the "Control Knob" to select "Sous Vide" mode.
4. Press "Timer Button" and rotate the "Control Knob" to set the time for 20 minutes.
5. Now press "Temp Button" and rotate the "Control Knob" to set the temperature to 185 degrees F.
6. Close the Power XL Grill Air Fryer Combo with "Glass Lid" and press "Start Button" to preheat.
7. Meanwhile, in a food processor, add all ingredients except for corn and salt and pulse till smooth.
8. In a cooking pouch, place corn and butter mixture.
9. Seal the pouch tightly after squeezing out the excess air.
10. When the unit shows "Add Food", open the lid and place the pouch in inner pot.
11. Close the lid and press "Start Button" to start cooking.
12. Meanwhile, preheat the broiler of oven to high.
13. When the cooking time is completed, press "Cancel Button" to stop cooking.
14. Open the lid and remove the pouch from inner pot.
15. Carefully open the pouch and remove corn ears from pouch.
16. Arrange corn ears onto a baking sheet and broil for about 2 minutes.
17. Serve immediately.

Nutritional Information per Serving:

- Calories 227
- Total Fat 9.6 g
- Saturated Fat 5.2 g
- Cholesterol 20 mg
- Sodium 833 mg
- Total Carbs 34.4 g
- Fiber 4.4 g
- Sugar 9.3 g

- Protein 6.4 g

Potato Fries

Preparation Time: 15 minutes
Cooking Time: 16 minutes
Servings: 2

Ingredients:

- ½ pound potatoes, peeled and cut into ½-inch thick sticks lengthwise
- 1 tablespoon olive oil
- Salt and ground black pepper, as required

Method:

1. In a large bowl, add all the ingredients and toss to coat well.
2. Plug in the Power XL Grill Air Fryer Combo.
3. Rotate the "Control Knob" to select "Air Fry" mode.
4. Press "Timer Button" and rotate the "Control Knob" to set the time for 16 minutes.
5. Now press "Temp Button" and rotate the "Control Knob" to set the temperature to 400 degrees F.
6. Close the Power XL Grill Air Fryer Combo with "Air Frying Lid" and press "Start Button" to preheat.
7. When the unit shows "Add Food", open the lid and arrange the potato sticks into the greased inner pot.
8. Close the lid and press "Start Button" to start cooking.
9. Flip the potato sticks once halfway through.
10. When the cooking time is completed, press "Cancel Button" to stop cooking.
11. Open the lid and serve warm.

Nutritional Information per Serving:

- Calories 138
- Total Fat 7.1 g
- Saturated Fat 1 g
- Cholesterol 0 mg
- Sodium 84 mg
- Total Carbs 17.8 g
- Fiber 2.7 g
- Sugar 1.3 g
- Protein 1.9 g

Zucchini Fries

Preparation Time: 10 minutes
Cooking Time: 10 minutes
Servings: 6

Ingredients:

- 1 pound zucchini, sliced into 2½-inch sticks
- Salt, as required
- 2 tablespoons olive oil
- ¾ cup breadcrumbs

Method:

1. In a colander, add the zucchini and sprinkle with salt.
2. Set aside for about 10 minutes.
3. Gently pat dry the zucchini sticks with the paper towels and coat with oil.
4. In a shallow dish, place the breadcrumbs.
5. Coat the zucchini sticks with the breadcrumbs evenly.
6. Plug in the Power XL Grill Air Fryer Combo.
7. Rotate the "Control Knob" to select "Air Fry" mode.
8. Press "Timer Button" and rotate the "Control Knob" to set the time for 10 minutes.
9. Now press "Temp Button" and rotate the "Control Knob" to set the temperature to 425 degrees F.
10. Close the Power XL Grill Air Fryer Combo with "Air Frying Lid" and press "Start Button" to preheat.
11. When unit shows "Add Food", open the lid and arrange the zucchini sticks into the greased inner pot.
12. Close the lid and press "Start Button" to start cooking.
13. When the cooking time is completed, press "Cancel Button" to stop cooking.
14. Open the lid and serve warm.

Nutritional Information per Serving:

- Calories 105
- Total Fat 5.5 g
- Saturated Fat 0.9 g
- Cholesterol 0 mg
- Sodium 134 mg
- Total Carbs 12.3 g
- Fiber 1.4 g
- Sugar 2.2 g
- Protein 2.7 g

Jalapeño Poppers

Preparation Time: 15 minutes
Cooking Time: 13 minutes
Servings: 6

Ingredients:

- 12 large jalapeño peppers
- 8 ounces cream cheese, softened
- ¼ cup scallion, chopped
- ¼ cup fresh cilantro, chopped
- ¼ teaspoon onion powder
- ¼ teaspoon garlic powder
- Salt, as required
- 1/3 cup sharp cheddar cheese, grated

Method:

1. Carefully, cut off one-third of each pepper lengthwise and then, scoop out the seeds and membranes.
2. In a bowl, mix together the cream cheese, scallion, cilantro, spices and salt.
3. Stuff each pepper with the cream cheese mixture and top with cheese.
4. Plug in the Power XL Grill Air Fryer Combo.
5. Rotate the "Control Knob" to select "Air Fry" mode.
6. Press "Timer Button" and rotate the "Control Knob" to set the time for 13 minutes.
7. Now press "Temp Button" and rotate the "Control Knob" to set the temperature to 400 degrees F.
8. Close the Power XL Grill Air Fryer Combo with "Air Frying Lid" and press "Start Button" to preheat.
9. When unit shows "Add Food", open the lid and arrange the jalapeño peppers into the greased inner pot.
10. Close the lid and press "Start Button" to start cooking.
11. When the cooking time is completed, press "Cancel Button" to stop cooking.
12. Open the lid and serve immediately.

Nutritional Information per Serving:

- Calories 171
- Total Fat 15.7 g
- Saturated Fat 9.7 g
- Cholesterol 45 mg
- Sodium 914 mg
- Total Carbs 3.7 g
- Fiber 1.3 g
- Sugar 1.2 g
- Protein 4.9 g

Buffalo Chicken Wings

Preparation Time: 10 minutes
Cooking Time: 16 minutes
Servings: 5

Ingredients:

- 2 pounds frozen chicken wings, drums and flats separated
- 2 tablespoons olive oil
- 2 tablespoons Buffalo sauce
- ½ teaspoon red pepper flakes, crushed
- Salt, as required

Method:

1. Coat the chicken wings with oil evenly.
2. Plug in the Power XL Grill Air Fryer Combo.
3. Rotate the "Control Knob" to select "Air Fry" mode.
4. Press "Timer Button" and rotate the "Control Knob" to set the time for 16 minutes.
5. Now press "Temp Button" and rotate the "Control Knob" to set the temperature to 390 degrees F.
6. Close the Power XL Grill Air Fryer Combo with "Air Frying Lid" and press "Start Button" to preheat.
7. When the unit shows "Add Food", open the lid and arrange the chicken wings into the greased inner pot.
8. Close the lid and press "Start Button" to start cooking.
9. After 12 minutes of cooking, flip the wings and coat with barbecue sauce evenly.
10. Meanwhile, in a large bowl, add Buffalo sauce, red pepper flakes and salt and mix well.
11. When the cooking time is completed, press "Cancel Button" to stop cooking.
12. Open the lid and transfer the wings into a bowl.
13. Add the buffalo sauce and toss to coat well.
14. Serve immediately.

Nutritional Information per Serving:

- Calories 394
- Total Fat 19.1 g
- Saturated Fat 4.5 g
- Cholesterol 161 mg
- Sodium 224 mg
- Total Carbs 0.2 g
- Fiber 0.1 g
- Sugar 0 g

- Protein 52.6 g

Cod Nuggets

Preparation Time: 15 minutes
Cooking Time: 8 minutes
Servings: 6

Ingredients:

- 1 cup all-purpose flour
- 2 eggs
- ¾ cup seasoned breadcrumbs
- 2 tablespoons vegetable oil
- 1 pound boneless cod fillet, cut into strips

Method:

1. In a shallow plate, place the flour.
2. In a second shallow plate, crack the eggs and beat well.
3. In a third shallow plate, mix together the breadcrumbs and oil.
4. Coat the nuggets with flour, then dip into beaten eggs and finally, coat with the breadcrumbs.
5. Plug in the Power XL Grill Air Fryer Combo.
6. Rotate the "Control Knob" to select "Air Fry" mode.
7. Press "Timer Button" and rotate the "Control Knob" to set the time for 8 minutes.
8. Now press "Temp Button" and rotate the "Control Knob" to set the temperature to 390 degrees F.
9. Close the Power XL Grill Air Fryer Combo with "Air Frying Lid" and press "Start Button" to preheat.
10. When unit shows "Add Food", open the lid and arrange the nuggets into the greased inner pot.
11. Close the lid and press "Start Button" to start cooking.
12. When the cooking time is completed, press "Cancel Button" to stop cooking.
13. Open the lid and serve warm.

Nutritional Information per Serving:

- Calories 253
- Total Fat 8.6 g
- Saturated Fat 1.4 g
- Cholesterol 92 mg
- Sodium 243 mg
- Total Carbs 24.5 g
- Fiber 1.1 g
- Sugar 0.2 g
- Protein 19 g

Bacon Croquettes

Preparation Time: 15 minutes
Cooking Time: 8 minutes
Servings: 6

Ingredients:

- 1 pound thin bacon slices
- 1 pound sharp Cheddar cheese block, cut into 1-inch rectangular pieces
- 1 cup flour
- 3 eggs
- 1 cup breadcrumbs
- Salt, as required
- ¼ cup olive oil

Method:

1. Wrap 2 bacon slices around 1 piece of Cheddar cheese, covering completely.
2. Repeat with the remaining bacon and cheese pieces.
3. Plug in the Power XL Grill Air Fryer Combo.
4. Rotate the "Control Knob" to select "Air Fry" mode.
5. Press "Timer Button" and rotate the "Control Knob" to set the time for 8 minutes.
6. Now press "Temp Button" and rotate the "Control Knob" to set the temperature to 390 degrees F.
7. Close the Power XL Grill Air Fryer Combo with "Air Frying Lid" and press "Start Button" to preheat.
8. When unit shows "Add Food", open the lid and arrange the croquettes into the greased inner pot.
9. Close the lid and press "Start Button" to start cooking.
10. When the cooking time is completed, press "Cancel Button" to stop cooking.
11. Open the lid and serve warm.

Nutritional Information per Serving:

- Calories 567
- Total Fat 37.1 g
- Saturated Fat 18.1 g
- Cholesterol 161 mg
- Sodium 703 mg
- Total Carbs 30 g
- Fiber 1.4 g
- Sugar 1.7 g
- Protein 26.1 g

Crumbed Shrimp

Preparation Time: 20 minutes
Cooking Time: 20 minutes
Servings: 6

Ingredients:

- 8 ounces coconut milk
- Salt and ground black pepper, as required
- ½ cup panko breadcrumbs
- ½ teaspoon cayenne pepper
- 1 pound shrimp, peeled and deveined

Method:

1. In a shallow dish, mix together the coconut milk, salt and black pepper.
2. In another shallow dish, mix together breadcrumbs, cayenne pepper, salt and black pepper.
3. Dip the shrimp in coconut milk mixture and then coat with the breadcrumb mixture.
4. Plug in the Power XL Grill Air Fryer Combo.
5. Rotate the "Control Knob" to select "Air Fry" mode.
6. Press "Timer Button" and rotate the "Control Knob" to set the time for 20 minutes.
7. Now press "Temp Button" and rotate the "Control Knob" to set the temperature to 350 degrees F.
8. Close the Power XL Grill Air Fryer Combo with "Air Frying Lid" and press "Start Button" to preheat.
9. When unit shows "Add Food", open the lid and arrange the shrimp into the greased inner pot.
10. Close the lid and press "Start Button" to start cooking.
11. When the cooking time is completed, press "Cancel Button" to stop cooking.
12. Open the lid and serve warm.

Nutritional Information per Serving:

- Calories 187
- Total Fat 10.3 g
- Saturated Fat 8.2 g
- Cholesterol 120 mg
- Sodium ˋ20 mg
- Total Carbs 3.5 g
- Fiber 0.9 g
- Sugar 1.3 g
- Protein 16.4 g

Bacon-Wrapped Prawns

Preparation Time: 15 minutes
Cooking Time: 7 minutes
Servings: 6

Ingredients:

- 1 pound bacon, thinly sliced
- 1 pound prawns, peeled and deveined

Method:

1. Wrap each prawn with one bacon slice.
2. Arrange the prawns into the baking pan and refrigerate for about 20 minutes.
3. Plug in the Power XL Grill Air Fryer Combo.
4. Rotate the "Control Knob" to select "Air Fry" mode.
5. Press "Timer Button" and rotate the "Control Knob" to set the time for 7 minutes.
6. Now press "Temp Button" and rotate the "Control Knob" to set the temperature to 390 degrees F.
7. Close the Power XL Grill Air Fryer Combo with "Air Frying Lid" and press "Start Button" to preheat.
8. When unit shows "Add Food", open the lid and arrange the prawns into the greased inner pot.
9. Close the lid and press "Start Button" to start cooking.
10. When the cooking time is completed, press "Cancel Button" to stop cooking.
11. Open the lid and serve warm.

Nutritional Information per Serving:

- Calories 456
- Total Fat 31.6 g
- Saturated Fat 10.4 g
- Cholesterol 83 mg
- Sodium 1334 mg
- Total Carbs 1.1 g
- Fiber 0 g
- Sugar 0 g
- Protein 38.6 g

Cauliflower Hummus

Preparation Time: 15 minutes
Cooking Time: 1½ hours
Servings: 8

Ingredients:

- 4 cups cauliflower, chopped
- 2 cups water
- 2/3 cup raw cashews
- 2 garlic cloves, peeled
- ½ teaspoon dried basil
- ½ teaspoon dried oregano
- ½ teaspoon dried rosemary
- ¼ cup nutritional yeast
- Salt and ground black pepper, as required

Method:

1. Plug in the Power XL Grill Air Fryer Combo.
2. Fill the inner pot with water.
3. Rotate the "Control Knob" to select "Sous Vide" mode.
4. Press "Timer Button" and rotate the "Control Knob" to set the time for 1½ hours.
5. Now press "Temp Button" and rotate the "Control Knob" to set the temperature to 185 degrees F.
6. Close the Power XL Grill Air Fryer Combo with "Glass Lid" and press "Start Button" to preheat.
7. Meanwhile, in a cooking pouch, place the cauliflower, water cashews, garlic and herbs.
8. Seal the pouch tightly after squeezing out the excess air.
9. When the unit shows "Add Food", open the lid and place the pouch in inner pot.
10. Close the lid and press "Start Button" to start cooking.
11. When the cooking time is completed, press "Cancel Button" to stop cooking.
12. Open the lid and remove the pouch from inner pot.
13. Carefully open the pouch and remove the cauliflower mixture.
14. Transfer the cauliflower mixture into a blender and pulse till smooth.
15. Serve immediately.

Nutritional Information per Serving:

- Calories 97
- Total Fat 5.6 g
- Saturated Fat 1.1 g
- Cholesterol 0 mg
- Sodium 41 mg
- Total Carbs 9 g
- Fiber 2.9 g
- Sugar 1.8 g
- Protein 5.1 g

Queso Blanco Dip

Preparation Time: 10 minutes
Cooking Time: 30 minutes
Servings: 10

Ingredients:

- 1½ cups Chihuahua cheese, shredded finely
- ¼ cup half-and-half
- 4 ounces green chilies, chopped
- 1 Serrano pepper, stemmed and chopped finely
- 2 tablespoons onion, grated
- 2 teaspoons ground cumin
- ½ teaspoon salt

Method:

1. Plug in the Power XL Grill Air Fryer Combo.
2. Fill the inner pot with water.
3. Rotate the "Control Knob" to select "Sous Vide" mode.
4. Press "Timer Button" and rotate the "Control Knob" to set the time for 30 minutes.
5. Now press "Temp Button" and rotate the "Control Knob" to set the temperature to 175 degrees F.
6. Close the Power XL Grill Air Fryer Combo with "Glass Lid" and press "Start Button" to preheat.
7. Meanwhile, in a cooking pouch, place all ingredients.
8. Seal the pouch tightly after squeezing out the excess air.
9. When the unit shows "Add Food", open the lid and place the pouch in inner pot.
10. Close the lid and press "Start Button" to start cooking.
11. When the cooking time is completed, press "Cancel Button" to stop cooking.
12. Open the lid and remove the pouch from inner pot.
13. Carefully open the pouch and immediately, transfer dip into a bowl.
14. Serve hot.

Nutritional Information per Serving:

- Calories 111
- Total Fat 6.5 g
- Saturated Fat 3.7 g
- Cholesterol 20 mg
- Sodium 2354 mg
- Total Carbs 9.5 g
- Fiber 3.4 g
- Sugar 5.7 g
- Protein 5.1 g

Beef Dip

Preparation Time: 15 minutes
Cooking Time: 2 hours 5 minutes
Servings: 20

Ingredients:

- 1 teaspoon olive oil
- 2 pounds lean ground beef
- 1 cup yellow onion, chopped
- 2 garlic cloves, minced
- 1 (4-ounce) can mild chile peppers, chopped
- 2 (6-ounce) cans tomato sauce
- 16 ounces cream cheese, cubed
- ½ cup Parmesan cheese, grated
- ½ cup ketchup
- 1 teaspoon dried oregano
- 1½ teaspoons red chili powder
- ½ teaspoon ground cumin
- Salt and ground black pepper, as required

Method:

1. Plug in the Power XL Grill Air Fryer Combo and add the oil in the inner pot.
2. Rotate the "Control Knob" to select "Sauté" mode and press "Start Button" to start cooking.
3. Add the beef and cook for about 4-5 minutes, stirring frequently with a wooden spoon.
4. Press "Cancel Button" to stop cooking and remove the grease from the pot.
5. Rotate the "Control Knob" to select "Slow Cook" mode.
6. Press "Timer Button" and rotate the "Control Knob" to set the time for 2 hours.
7. Close the Power XL Grill Air Fryer Combo with "Glass Lid" and press "Start Button" to start cooking.
8. When the cooking time is completed, press "Cancel Button" to stop cooking.
9. Open the lid and serve hot.

Nutritional Information per Serving:

- Calories 205
- Total Fat 12.7 g
- Saturated Fat 7.1 g
- Cholesterol 71 mg
- Sodium 438 mg
- Total Carbs 4.6 g
- Fiber 0.5 g
- Sugar 2.6 g
- Protein 18.3 g

Chapter 10: Dessert Recipes

Stuffed Apples

Preparation Time: 10 minutes
Cooking Time: 2 hours
Servings: 4

Ingredients:

- 4 tart apples
- 2 tablespoons fresh lemon juice
- 3 tablespoons unsalted butter
- 2 tablespoons light brown sugar
- 2 whole fresh dates, pitted and chopped
- 2 tablespoons raisins
- 1 teaspoon ground cinnamon
- ¼ teaspoons ground nutmeg
- ¼ teaspoons salt
- 1/8 teaspoons vanilla extract

Method:

1. Plug in the Power XL Grill Air Fryer Combo.
2. Fill the inner pot with water.
3. Rotate the "Control Knob" to select "Sous Vide" mode.
4. Press "Timer Button" and rotate the "Control Knob" to set the time for 2 hours.
5. Now press "Temp Button" and rotate the "Control Knob" to set the temperature to 183 degrees F.
6. Close the Power XL Grill Air Fryer Combo with "Glass Lid" and press "Start Button" to preheat.
7. Meanwhile, with a sharp knife, core the apples, leaving the base of the apple intact.
8. In a bowl, add the apples and lemon juice and gently toss to coat.
9. In another bowl, add butter, brown sugar, dates, raisins, spices, salt and vanilla and with a fork, mash until a chunky paste is formed.
10. Divide the filling in the center of each apple, pressing gently to compact the filling.
11. In 2 cooking pouches, divide the apples.
12. Seal the pouches tightly after squeezing out the excess air.
13. When the unit shows "Add Food", open the lid and place the pouch in inner pot.
14. Close the lid and press "Start Button" to start cooking.
15. When the cooking time is completed, press "Cancel Button" to stop cooking.
16. Open the lid and remove the pouches from inner pot.
17. Carefully open the pouches and transfer the apples onto the serving plates.
18. Serve warm.

Nutritional Information per Serving:

- Calories 239
- Total Fat 9.2 g
- Saturated Fat 5.6 g
- Cholesterol 23 mg
- Sodium 214 mg

- Total Carbs 42.6 g
- Fiber 6.3 g
- Sugar 33.1 g
- Protein 1 g

Poached Pears

Preparation Time: 10 minutes
Cooking Time: 2 hours
Servings: 4

Ingredients:

- 4 ripe pears, peeled
- 1 cup red wine
- ¼ cup sweet vermouth
- ½ cup granulated sugar
- 1 teaspoon salt
- 1 (3-inch) piece orange zest
- 1 vanilla bean, seeds scraped

Method:

1. Plug in the Power XL Grill Air Fryer Combo.
2. Fill the inner pot with water.
3. Rotate the "Control Knob" to select "Sous Vide" mode.
4. Press "Timer Button" and rotate the "Control Knob" to set the time for 1 hour.
5. Now press "Temp Button" and rotate the "Control Knob" to set the temperature to 175 degrees F.
6. Close the Power XL Grill Air Fryer Combo with "Glass Lid" and press "Start Button" to preheat.
7. Meanwhile, in a cooking pouch, place all ingredients.
8. Seal the pouch tightly after squeezing out the excess air.
9. When unit shows "Add Food", open the lid and place the pouch in inner pot.
10. Close the lid and press "Start Button" to start cooking.
11. When the cooking time is completed, press "Cancel Button" to stop cooking.
12. Open the lid and remove the pouch from inner pot.
13. Carefully open the pouch and transfer the pears onto serving plates.
14. Drizzle with some of the cooking liquid and serve.

Nutritional Information per Serving:

- Calories 276
- Total Fat 0.3 g
- Saturated Fat 0 g
- Cholesterol 0 mg
- Sodium 588 mg
- Total Carbs 59 g
- Fiber 6.5 g
- Sugar 46 g
- Protein 0.8 g

Chocolaty Strawberries

Preparation Time: 15 minutes
Cooking Time: 20 minutes
Servings: 6

Ingredients:

- 1 (12-ounce) package chocolate chips
- ½ teaspoon ground cinnamon
- 1/8 teaspoons cayenne pepper
- 1 cup fresh strawberries, hulled

Method:

1. Plug in the Power XL Grill Air Fryer Combo.
2. Fill the inner pot with water.
3. Rotate the "Control Knob" to select "Sous Vide" mode.
4. Press "Timer Button" and rotate the "Control Knob" to set the time for 10 minutes.
5. Now press "Temp Button" and rotate the "Control Knob" to set the temperature to 115 degrees F.
6. Close the Power XL Grill Air Fryer Combo with "Glass Lid" and press "Start Button" to preheat.
7. Meanwhile, in a cooking pouch, place the chocolate, cinnamon and cayenne pepper.
8. Seal the pouch tightly after squeezing out the excess air.
9. When unit shows "Add Food", open the lid and place the pouch in inner pot.
10. Close the lid and press "Start Button" to start cooking.
11. After 10 minutes of cooking, set the temperature to 90 degrees F for 10 minutes.
12. When the cooking time is completed, press "Cancel Button" to stop cooking.
13. Open the lid and remove the pouch from inner pot.
14. Carefully open the pouch and transfer the chocolate into a bowl.
15. Dip the strawberries in melted chocolate and transfer onto a wax paper-lined baking tray.
16. Refrigerate for at least 30 minutes or until set before serving.

Nutritional Information per Serving:

- Calories 312
- Total Fat 16.9 g
- Saturated Fat 11.8 g
- Cholesterol 13 mg
- Sodium 45 mg
- Total Carbs 305.7 g
- Fiber 2.5 g
- Sugar 30.4 g

- Protein 4.5 g

Honey Bourbon Cranberries

Preparation Time: 10 minutes
Cooking Time: 1 hour
Servings: 4

Ingredients:

- 1 cup honey
- 7½ ounces fresh cranberries
- ½ ounce bourbon
- 1 tablespoon orange zest

Method:

1. Plug in the Power XL Grill Air Fryer Combo.
2. Fill the inner pot with water.
3. Rotate the "Control Knob" to select "Sous Vide" mode.
4. Press "Timer Button" and rotate the "Control Knob" to set the time for 1 hour.
5. Now press "Temp Button" and rotate the "Control Knob" to set the temperature to 183 degrees F.
6. Close the Power XL Grill Air Fryer Combo with "Glass Lid" and press "Start Button" to preheat.
7. Meanwhile, in a cooking pouch, place all ingredients.
8. Seal the pouch tightly after squeezing out the excess air.
9. When unit shows "Add Food", open the lid and place the pouch in inner pot.
10. Close the lid and press "Start Button" to start cooking.
11. When the cooking time is completed, press "Cancel Button" to stop cooking.
12. Open the lid and remove the pouch from inner pot.
13. With a towel, smash the cranberries in the pouch.
14. Carefully open the pouch and transfer the cranberries into a bowl.
15. Serve warm.

Nutritional Information per Serving:

- Calories 296
- Total Fat 0 g
- Saturated Fat 0 g
- Cholesterol 0 mg
- Sodium 3 mg
- Total Carbs 75 g
- Fiber 2.3 g
- Sugar 71.5 g
- Protein 0.3 g

Chocolate Zabaglione

Preparation Time: 15 minutes
Cooking Time: 30 minutes
Servings: 8

Ingredients:

- 1 cup sugar
- ½ cup dry Marsala
- 8 large egg yolks
- Pinch of salt
- 1/3 cup unsweetened cocoa powder
- ¼ cup whipping cream
- 1 pound fresh strawberries, hulled and quartered

Method:

1. In a bowl, add sugar, Marsala, egg yolks and salt and beat until well combined.
2. Add the cocoa powder and beat until well combined.
3. Add the cream and beat well.
4. Plug in the Power XL Grill Air Fryer Combo.
5. Fill the inner pot with water.
6. Rotate the "Control Knob" to select "Sous Vide" mode.
7. Press "Timer Button" and rotate the "Control Knob" to set the time for 30 minutes.
8. Now press "Temp Button" and rotate the "Control Knob" to set the temperature to 165 degrees F.
9. Close the Power XL Grill Air Fryer Combo with "Glass Lid" and press "Start Button" to preheat.
10. Meanwhile, in a cooking pouch, place the egg mixture.
11. Seal the pouch tightly after squeezing out the excess air.
12. When unit shows "Add Food", open the lid and place the pouch in inner pot.
13. Close the lid and press "Start Button" to start cooking.
14. When the cooking time is completed, press "Cancel Button" to stop cooking.
15. Open the lid and remove the pouch from inner pot.
16. Carefully open the pouch and transfer the chocolate mixture into a owl.
17. Set aside to cool slightly.
18. Divide the strawberries into dessert bowls evenly.
19. Place warm zabaglione over the strawberries and refrigerate, covered to chill before serving.

Nutritional Information per Serving:

- Calories 197
- Total Fat 6.3 g
- Saturated Fat 2.6 g
- Cholesterol 214 mg
- Sodium 31 mg

- Total Carbs 32.4 g
- Fiber 2.3 g
- Sugar 28 g
- Protein 3.9 g

Raspberry Mousse

Preparation Time: 15 minutes
Cooking Time: 45 minutes
Servings: 8

Ingredients:

- 1 pound fresh raspberries
- ¼ cup ultrafine sugar
- 3 tablespoons fresh lemon juice
- ¼ teaspoons ground cinnamon
- ½ teaspoon salt
- 1 cup heavy cream
- 1 teaspoon vanilla extract

Method:

1. Plug in the Power XL Grill Air Fryer Combo.
2. Fill the inner pot with water.
3. Rotate the "Control Knob" to select "Sous Vide" mode.
4. Press "Timer Button" and rotate the "Control Knob" to set the time for 45 minutes.
5. Now press "Temp Button" and rotate the "Control Knob" to set the temperature to 180 degrees F.
6. Close the Power XL Grill Air Fryer Combo with "Glass Lid" and press "Start Button" to preheat.
7. Meanwhile, in a cooking pouch, place the raspberries, sugar, lemon juice, cinnamon and salt.
8. Seal the pouch tightly after squeezing out the excess air.
9. When unit shows "Add Food", open the lid and place the pouch in inner pot.
10. Close the lid and press "Start Button" to start cooking.
11. When the cooking time is completed, press "Cancel Button" to stop cooking.
15. Open the lid and remove the pouch from inner pot.
16. Immediately transfer the pouch into an ice bath to cool.
17. In a food processor, add the raspberry mixture and pulse until smooth.
18. Transfer into a bowl and keep aside to cool in room temperature.
19. In a large chilled mixing bowl, add the cream and vanilla and beat until stiff peaks form.
20. Gently fold in raspberry puree.
21. Refrigerate to chill before serving.

Nutritional Information per Serving:

- Calories 108
- Total Fat 6 g
- Saturated Fat 3.5 g
- Cholesterol 21 mg
- Sodium 155 mg

- Total Carbs 13.7 g
- Fiber 3.8 g
- Sugar 9 g
- Protein 1 g

Lemon Curd

Preparation Time: 10 minutes
Cooking Time: 1 hour
Servings: 4

Ingredients:

- ½ cup sugar
- 3 large eggs
- 4 tablespoons butter, melted
- ¼ cup fresh lemon juice
- 2 tablespoons lemon zest
- 1½ teaspoons gelatin

Method:

1. Plug in the Power XL Grill Air Fryer Combo.
2. Fill the inner pot with water.
3. Rotate the "Control Knob" to select "Sous Vide" mode.
4. Press "Timer Button" and rotate the "Control Knob" to set the time for 45-60 minutes.
5. Now press "Temp Button" and rotate the "Control Knob" to set the temperature to 165 degrees F.
6. Close the Power XL Grill Air Fryer Combo with "Glass Lid" and press "Start Button" to preheat.
7. Meanwhile, in a cooking pouch, place all ingredients.
8. Seal the pouch tightly after squeezing out the excess air.
9. When unit shows "Add Food", open the lid and place the pouch in inner pot.
10. Close the lid and press "Start Button" to start cooking.
11. When the cooking time is completed, press "Cancel Button" to stop cooking.
12. Open the lid and remove the pouch from inner pot.
13. Carefully open the pouch.
14. Transfer mixture into a blender and pulse until well combined and smooth.
15. Transfer the mixture into a bowl and set aside to cool.
16. Transfer into a container and refrigerate before using.

Nutritional Information per Serving:

- Calories 205
- Total Fat 12.3 g
- Saturated Fat 6.9 g
- Cholesterol 136 mg
- Sodium 110 mg
- Total Carbs 21.2 g
- Fiber 0.3 g
- Sugar 20.7 g
- Protein 4.1 g

Chocolate Fondue

Preparation Time: 10 minutes
Cooking Time: 1 hour
Servings: 8

Ingredients:

- 16 ounces dark chocolate, chopped
- 1 cup heavy cream
- 1 ounce brewed coffee
- ½ cup sugar
- ¼ teaspoons liquid stevia
- 1 teaspoon vanilla extract

Method:

1. Plug in the Power XL Grill Air Fryer Combo.
2. In the inner pot, add all the ingredients and stir to combine.
3. Rotate the "Control Knob" to select "Slow Cook" mode.
4. Press "Timer Button" and rotate the "Control Knob" to set the time for 1 hour.
5. Close the Power XL Grill Air Fryer Combo with "Glass Lid" and press "Start Button" to start cooking.
6. When the cooking time is completed, press "Cancel Button" to stop cooking.
7. Open the lid and transfer the mixture into a owl.
8. With a wire whisk, mix until smooth.
9. Serve warm.

Nutritional Information per Serving:

- Calories 404
- Total Fat 22.4 g
- Saturated Fat 15.2 g
- Cholesterol 34 mg
- Sodium 51 mg
- Total Carbs 46.7 g
- Fiber 1.9 g
- Sugar 41.7 g
- Protein 4.7 g

Blueberry Custard

Preparation Time: 15 minutes
Cooking Time: 3 hours
Servings: 6

Ingredients:

- 6 large eggs, separated
- 2 cups light cream
- ½ cup coconut flour
- ½ cup sugar
- 1/3 cup fresh lemon juice
- 2 teaspoons lemon zest, grated
- 1 teaspoon lemon liquid stevia
- ¼ teaspoon salt
- ½ cup fresh blueberries

Method:

1. In the bowl of a stand mixer, add the egg whites and beat until stiff peaks form. Set aside.
2. In another bowl, add the egg yolks and remaining ingredients except blueberries and beat until well combined.
3. Slowly, add the whipped egg whites, a little at a time and gently, mix until just combined.
4. Plug in the Power XL Grill Air Fryer Combo.
5. In the inner pot, place the egg mixture and sprinkle with the blueberries.
6. Rotate the "Control Knob" to select "Slow Cook" mode.
7. Press "Timer Button" and rotate the "Control Knob" to set the time for 3 hours.
8. Close the Power XL Grill Air Fryer Combo with "Glass Lid" and press "Start Button" to start cooking.
9. When the cooking time is completed, press "Cancel Button" to stop cooking.
10. Open the lid and transfer the custard into a large bowl.
11. Set aside to cool.
12. Refrigerate for about 2 hours before serving.

Nutritional Information per Serving:

- Calories 266
- Total Fat 17.7 g
- Saturated Fat 9.6 g
- Cholesterol 230 mg
- Sodium 283 mg
- Total Carbs 21.1 g
- Fiber 0.8 g
- Sugar 18.7 g
- Protein 7.6 g

Pumpkin Custard

Preparation Time: 15 minutes
Cooking Time: 2½ hours
Servings: 6

Ingredients:

- 4 large eggs
- ½ cup sugar
- 1 cup pumpkin puree
- 1 teaspoon organic vanilla extract
- ½ cup almond flour
- 1 teaspoon pumpkin pie spice
- 1/8 teaspoons salt
- 4 tablespoons butter, melted

Method:

1. In a bowl, add the eggs and with an electric mixer, beat until smooth and slightly thickened.
2. Slowly, add the Erythritol, beating continuously until well combined.
3. Add pumpkin puree and vanilla extract and beat until well combined.
4. Add the almond flour, pumpkin pie spice and salt and beat until well combined.
5. Slowly, add the melted butter, beating continuously until well combined.
6. Plug in the Power XL Grill Air Fryer Combo.
7. In the greased inner pot, place the pumpkin mixture evenly.
8. Rotate the "Control Knob" to select "Slow Cook" mode.
9. Press "Timer Button" and rotate the "Control Knob" to set the time for 2-2½ hours.
10. Close the Power XL Grill Air Fryer Combo with "Glass Lid" and press "Start Button" to start cooking.
11. When the cooking time is completed, press "Cancel Button" to stop cooking.
12. Open the lid and serve warm.

Nutritional Information per Serving:

- Calories 195
- Total Fat 15.6 g
- Saturated Fat 6.3 g
- Cholesterol 145 mg
- Sodium 157 mg
- Total Carbs 22.5 g
- Fiber 2.2 g
- Sugar 18.4 g
- Protein 6.7 g

Chocolate Pudding

Preparation Time: 15 minutes
Cooking Time: 30 minutes
Servings: 4

Ingredients:

- 3 eggs
- 2 egg yolks
- 1 cup milk
- ½ cup sugar
- ¼ cup cocoa powder
- ½ cup bittersweet chocolate chips
- 1 cup heavy cream

Method:

1. In a medium bowl, add eggs and yolks and beat well. Add milk and cream and beat until well combined. Add sugar and beat till well combined.
2. In another small bowl, add cocoa powder and a few tablespoons of egg mixture and beat until smooth.
3. Add cocoa mixture into remaining egg mixture and mix well.
4. Plug in the Power XL Grill Air Fryer Combo.
5. Fill the inner pot with water.
6. Rotate the "Control Knob" to select "Sous Vide" mode.
7. Press "Timer Button" and rotate the "Control Knob" to set the time for 20-30 minutes.
8. Now press "Temp Button" and rotate the "Control Knob" to set the temperature to 180 degrees F.
9. Close the Power XL Grill Air Fryer Combo with "Glass Lid" and press "Start Button" to preheat.
10. Meanwhile, in a cooking pouch, place the egg mixture with chocolate chips.
11. Seal the pouch tightly after squeezing out the excess air.
12. When unit shows "Add Food", open the lid and place the pouch in inner pot.
13. Close the lid and press "Start Button" to start cooking.
14. When the cooking time is completed, press "Cancel Button" to stop cooking.
15. Open the lid and remove the pouch from inner pot.
16. Immediately plunge the pouch into a large bowl of ice water for about 1-2 minutes.
17. With your fingers, knead pouch slightly and return into ice water to cool completely.
18. After cooling, open the pouch.
19. Transfer the mixture into a food processor and pulse until smooth.

20. Transfer the pudding into a serving bowl.

21. With a plastic wrap, cover the bowl and refrigerate before serving.

22. Serve with the topping of cream.

Nutritional Information per Serving:

- Calories 426
- Total Fat 24.8 g
- Saturated Fat 14.3 g
- Cholesterol 279 mg
- Sodium 108 mg

- Total Carbs 44.8 g
- Fiber 2.3 g
- Sugar 39 g
- Protein 10.7 g

Raisin Rice Pudding

Preparation Time: 10 minutes
Cooking Time: 2 hours
Servings: 10

Ingredients:

- 3 cups skim milk
- 2 cups Arborio rice
- ½ cup maple syrup
- ½ cup golden raisins
- 1 tablespoon butter
- 2 teaspoons ground cinnamon
- ½ teaspoon ground ginger

Method:

1. Plug in the Power XL Grill Air Fryer Combo.
2. Fill the inner pot with water.
3. Rotate the "Control Knob" to select "Sous Vide" mode.
4. Press "Timer Button" and rotate the "Control Knob" to set the time for 2 hours.
5. Now press "Temp Button" and rotate the "Control Knob" to set the temperature to 180 degrees F.
6. Close the Power XL Grill Air Fryer Combo with "Glass Lid" and press "Start Button" to preheat.
7. Meanwhile, in a cooking pouch, place all ingredients.
8. Seal the pouch tightly after squeezing out the excess air.
9. When unit shows "Add Food", open the lid and place the pouch in inner pot.
10. Close the lid and press "Start Button" to start cooking.
11. When the cooking time is completed, press "Cancel Button" to stop cooking.
12. Open the lid and remove the pouch from inner pot.
13. Carefully open the pouch and transfer rice mixture into a serving bowl.
14. With a fork, fluff the rice and serve.

Nutritional Information per Serving:

- Calories 238
- Total Fat 1.4 g
- Saturated Fat 0.8 g
- Cholesterol 5 mg
- Sodium 52 mg
- Total Carbs 50.6 g
- Fiber 1.6 g
- Sugar 17.3 g
- Protein 5.2 g

Strawberry Crumble

Preparation Time: 10 minutes
Cooking Time: 2 hours
Servings: 8

Ingredients:

- 2 cups almond flour
- 4 tablespoons butter, melted
- 12-16 drops liquid stevia
- 6-7 cups fresh strawberries, hulled and sliced
- 2 tablespoons butter, chopped

Method:

1. In a bowl, add the flour, melted butter and stevia and mix until a crumbly mixture forms.
2. Plug in the Power XL Grill Air Fryer Combo.
3. In the inner pot, place the strawberry slices and dot with chopped butter.
4. Spread the flour mixture on top evenly.
5. Rotate the "Control Knob" to select "Slow Cook" mode.
6. Press "Timer Button" and rotate the "Control Knob" to set the time for 2 hours.
7. Close the Power XL Grill Air Fryer Combo with "Glass Lid" and press "Start Button" to start cooking.
8. When the cooking time is completed, press "Cancel Button" to stop cooking.
9. Open the lid and serve warm.

Nutritional Information per Serving:

- Calories 279
- Total Fat 22.3 g
- Saturated Fat 6.5 g
- Cholesterol 23 mg
- Sodium 72 mg
- Total Carbs 14.3 g
- Fiber 5.2 g
- Sugar 5.3 g
- Protein 6.8 g

Peach Cobbler

Preparation Time: 10 minutes
Cooking Time: 8 hours
Servings: 8

Ingredients:

- ¾ cup bisquick mix
- 1/3 cup granulated sugar
- ½ cup brown sugar
- 2 large eggs, beaten
- 2 teaspoons vanilla extract
- 2 teaspoons butter, melted
- ½ cup evaporated milk
- 1 cup peaches, peeled, pitted and mashed
- ¾ teaspoon ground cinnamon

Method:

1. In a large mixing bowl, mix together bisquick, granulated sugar and brown sugar.
2. Add eggs, vanilla extract, butter and milk and mix until well combined.
3. Add peaches and cinnamon and mix well.
4. Plug in the Power XL Grill Air Fryer Combo.
5. In the inner pot, place the peach mixture.
6. Rotate the "Control Knob" to select "Slow Cook" mode.
7. Press "Timer Button" and rotate the "Control Knob" to set the time for 8 hours.
8. Close the Power XL Grill Air Fryer Combo with "Glass Lid" and press "Start Button" to start cooking.
9. When the cooking time is completed, press "Cancel Button" to stop cooking.
10. Open the lid and serve warm.

Nutritional Information per Serving:

- Calories 170
- Total Fat 5.2 g
- Saturated Fat 2.2 g
- Cholesterol 54 mg
- Sodium 183 mg
- Total Carbs 28.3 g
- Fiber 0.4 g
- Sugar 21 g
- Protein 3.7 g

Raspberry Cobbler

Preparation Time: 10 minutes
Cooking Time: 2 hours
Servings: 8

Ingredients:

- 1 cup almond flour
- ¼ cup coconut flour
- ¾ cup sugar
- 1 teaspoon baking soda
- 1/3 teaspoon ground cinnamon
- 1/8 teaspoon salt
- ¼ cup unsweetened coconut milk
- 2 tablespoons coconut oil
- 1 large egg, beaten lightly
- 4 cups fresh raspberries

Method:

1. In a large bowl, mix together the flours, sugar, baking soda, cinnamon and salt.
2. In another bowl, add the coconut milk, coconut oil and egg and beat until well combined.
3. Add the egg mixture into the flour mixture and mix until just combined.
4. Plug in the Power XL Grill Air Fryer Combo.
5. In the inner pot, place the egg mixture evenly and top with raspberries.
6. Rotate the "Control Knob" to select "Slow Cook" mode.
7. Press "Timer Button" and rotate the "Control Knob" to set the time for 2 hours.
8. Close the Power XL Grill Air Fryer Combo with "Glass Lid" and press "Start Button" to start cooking.
9. When the cooking time is completed, press "Cancel Button" to stop cooking.
10. Open the lid and serve warm.

Nutritional Information per Serving:

- Calories 180
- Total Fat 8 g
- Saturated Fat 4.9 g
- Cholesterol 23 mg
- Sodium 206 mg
- Total Carbs 27.6 g
- Fiber 4.8 g
- Sugar 21.9 g
- Protein 2.5 g

Chapter 11: 30 Days Meal Plan

Day 1

Breakfast: Oats Granola

Lunch: Beet & Feta Salad

Dinner: Sweet & Sour Cod

Day 2

Breakfast: Sweet Potato Porridge

Lunch: Vanilla & Paprika Shrimp

Dinner: Beef & Spinach Soup

Day 3

Breakfast: Zucchini Omelet

Lunch: Veggie Lasagna

Dinner: Halibut in Herb Sauce

Day 4

Breakfast: Artichoke Frittata

Lunch: Herbed Bell Peppers

Dinner: Pork with Apple

Day 5

Breakfast: Sausage & Mushroom Casserole

Lunch: Cauliflower Soup

Dinner: Chicken & Strawberry Salad

Day 6

Breakfast: Squash & Apple Porridge

Lunch: Pork Sausage & Oats Pilaf

Dinner: Lamb & Beans Chili

Day 7

Breakfast: Quinoa Porridge

Lunch: Potato Salad

Dinner: Buttered Turkey Breast

Day 8

Breakfast: Carrot Oatmeal

Lunch: Shrimp with Bell peppers

Dinner: Bacon-Wrapped Chicken Breasts

Day 9

Breakfast: Ham & Veggie Casserole

Lunch: Mushrooms in Sauce

Dinner: Glazed Pork Tenderloin

Day 10

Breakfast: Eggs with Turkey

Lunch: Zucchinis with Tomatoes

Dinner: Chicken with Beans

Day 11

Breakfast: Bacon & Kale Frittata

Lunch: Tomato Soup

Dinner: Beef Roast with Carrots

Day 12

Breakfast: Barley Porridge

Lunch: Cheesy Spinach

Dinner: Buttered Salmon

Day 13

Breakfast: Oats Granola

Lunch: Cheesy Macaroni

Dinner: Lamb Stew

Day 14

Breakfast: Squash & Apple Porridge

Lunch: Tomato Soup

Dinner: Turkey & Beans Chili

Day 15

Breakfast: Zucchini Omelet

Lunch: Buttered Scallops

Dinner: Lemony Beef Roast

Day 16

Breakfast: Wheat Berries Porridge

Lunch: Potato Salad

Dinner: Herbed Whole Chicken

Day 17

Breakfast: Artichoke Frittata

Lunch: Cheesy Macaroni

Dinner: Trout Salad

Day 18

Breakfast: Quinoa Porridge

Lunch: Zucchini with Tomatoes

Dinner: Spicy Pork Roast

Day 19

Breakfast: Simple Oatmeal

Lunch: Broccoli in Cheesy Sauce

Dinner: Citrus Turkey Legs

Day 20

Breakfast: Bacon & Kale Frittata

Lunch: Curried Cauliflower

Dinner: Beef Salad

Day 21

Breakfast: Ham & Veggie Casserole

Lunch: Mushrooms in Sauce

Dinner: Salmon & Veggie Stew

Day 22

Breakfast: Cheese Omelet

Lunch: Garlicky Butter Shrimp

Dinner: Garlicky Leg of Lamb

Day 23

Breakfast: Sausage & Mushroom Casserole

Lunch: Garlicky Brussels Sprout

Dinner: Cajun Herring

Day 24

Breakfast: Carrot Oatmeal

Lunch: Cauliflower Soup

Dinner: Thyme Beef Brisket

Day 25

Breakfast: Wheat Berries Porridge

Lunch: Garlicky Butter Shrimp

Dinner: Gingered Chicken Drumsticks

Day 26

Breakfast: Eggs with Turkey

Lunch: Cheesy Spinach

Dinner: Pork & Veggie Soup

Day 27

Breakfast: Barley Porridge

Lunch: Squash with Fruit

Dinner: Pork Meatballs in Tomato Gravy

Day 28

Breakfast: Cheese Omelet

Lunch: Pork Sausage & Oats Pilaf

Dinner: Seafood Soup

Day 29

Breakfast: Sweet Potato Porridge

Lunch: Broccoli Soup

Dinner: Lamb & Apricot Casserole

Day 30

Breakfast: Simple Oatmeal

Lunch: Buttered Scallops

Dinner: Chicken & Carrot Stew

Conclusion

PowerXL Grill is a revolution in the grill market, which can bring great convenience to the people who want to cook large portions of food at a time. The smart cooking modes of the PowerXL Grill is the greatest cooking advantage one can have; it makes it unbeatable when compared to another grill. If you have already brought this beauty home, then give it a try and put its 12 smart programs to test using the variety of recipes shared in this cookbook. Bring flavors to your routine menu and cook good food with convenience in the PowerXL Grill now.

Printed in Great Britain
by Amazon

28143343R00090